A
CERTAIN
SOMEWHERE

⟦A⟧

CERTAIN
SOMEWHERE

Writers on the Places
They Remember

EDITED BY ROBERT WILSON

RANDOM HOUSE

NEW YORK

Library of Congress Cataloging-in-Publication Data

A certain somewhere: writers on the places they remember / edited by Robert
Wilson.
p. cm.
ISBN 0-375-50849-X
1. United States—Description and travel—Anecdotes.   2. Voyages and
travels—Anecdotes.   3. Authors—Travel—United States—Anecdotes.
4. Authors—Travel—Anecdotes.   5. Travelers' writings.   I. Wilson, Robert

E169.04.C43   2002   222.3'159—dc21   2002020683

040903-2196 D8

Preface

IX YEARS AGO, *HISTORIC PRESERVATION* MAGAZINE dropped the word *historic* from its title and undertook a mild metamorphosis. With the encouragement of Richard Moe, the president of the National Trust for Historic Preservation, whose publication *Preservation* is, we sought to broaden the magazine's view, to look for subject matter that goes beyond what we on the staff thought of, perhaps uncharitably, as old houses for old ladies. The magazine would not just be about great mansions and historic landmarks, about the reglazing of crumbling windows or the chipping away of fourteen layers of lead paint. Our subjects would be history and architecture, true, but also the rebirth of cities, the reclamation of neighborhoods, travel, ideas, and the passions of people with a cause, the cause of making better places to live and work. One of our goals for what we considered to be a new publication was to bring into its pages writers with distinctive voices. But how? I've come to believe that the preservation instinct—the need to think carefully about what has been left to us and what we'll leave behind—eventually emerges in most people. But preservation itself is not a word or a concept guaranteed to make the heart leap up, at least not the hearts of the sorts of writers we were aiming for. We believed that the more congenial idea of place, which is closely connected to preservation (preservation being one of the ways to protect places we love or to reinvent places we don't)—is an idea no writer, or reader, can easily resist. In the introductory essay that follows, my friend and colleague Sudip Bose gets to the heart of why that is.

The years since this new beginning for the magazine have made us grateful for the number and variety of writers who have answered our call. They include novelists, journalists, poets, historians, critics, and one charming professor emeritus of linguistics at MIT. As you'll see, all of them can fairly be called essayists. We've been pleased, too, by how well the subject of place has held up. As each of us becomes ever more deeply entangled in the Web, as we spend more and more of our time in the placeless worlds of our office networks and hard drives, the lure of the physical world only grows. We come from the earth, after all, and will return to it. Our connection to the earth and what we build upon it is profound, as profound and mysterious as our connections to each other. September 11, 2001, can only deepen our realization that the permanence of any place anywhere cannot be taken for granted. The months since that day have taught us the related lesson that there is solace in what does last. More often than not, though, the essays collected here suggest that our connection to place is not touched by sorrow so much as by joy, often an exuberant joy.

My thanks to Sudip Bose for assigning and editing many of these essays, and for pulling together the original manuscript of this book. Thanks, too, to our colleagues Kim Keister, Allen Freeman, and Arnold Berke for their contributions. I thank Mary Bahr at Random House for the enthusiasm with which she helped conceive this book, and Random House publisher Ann Godoff for her warm support.

ROBERT WILSON

Contents

Introduction

SUDIP BOSE

N JULY 1996, *PRESERVATION* MAGAZINE BEGAN PUBLISHING A series of essays under the general title "Place," in the hope of better understanding what it is about a place that makes it mysterious and meaningful and worthy of contemplation. In keeping with the subject matter of our magazine, we limited ourselves to the built environment—buildings, monuments, parks, neighborhoods, villages, cities. Of course, any reader of Victorian poetry will know that the splendors of the natural world have inspired much great writing; a panorama of mountain peaks or the repose of a glade abuzz with bees or the sea, both tumultuous and placid, can move the human heart. But the beautiful and the divine also exist in that which is forged, fired, smelted, hammered out, erected, stacked, sweated over—created, in other words, by our own hands.

I think the late Eudora Welty had it right when she wrote in 1956 of the mystery of place in fiction: "Where does this mystery lie? Is it in the fact that place has a more lasting identity than we have, and we unswervingly tend to attach ourselves to identity? Might the magic lie partly, too, in the *name* of the place—since that is what *we* gave it? Surely, once we have it named, we have put a kind of poetic claim on its existence." And don't the places we inhabit claim something of us, too? In the essays in this collection, you will see just how strongly our identities can become a part of our structures. I'm thinking now of the walls on Noel Perrin's Vermont property, for example, built of thousands of granite stones that are both functional and appealing. And the New York Public Library, where Thomas Mallon has spent countless hours, a place so noble and elevating that it just had to insinuate itself into a few of his books. And a small cottage in Maui, described by Reeve Lindbergh, where her father, Charles, so long associated with the life of adventure and voyage, chose to live out his last days, crossing an ocean for the last time in order to get there.

Our presence upon the earth is brief, but the places we live among, the houses where we dwell, the courthouses that stand on village lawns, the strong bridges that accommodate our cars, the statues we put up to heroes of the past—these things, we like to think, ever optimistic, will endure. But will they? Ours is a society that values change, more at times even than stability; we become restless with the overly familiar. And so, all too often perhaps, we demolish the things we have built. That ballpark or apartment complex we once gazed upon with pride now strikes us as outdated, useless, unfamiliar. And yet we wince, at the very least, when a stately old building, showing its age but beautiful in spite of it (or, more likely, because of it), is bulldozed to make room for something new. Is it simply that we are sorry to witness the loss of something that has for so long delighted our eyes, or do we feel a deeper loss because we have attached ourselves, our identities, to it?

These essays instruct (as they delight), because they show their authors trying to figure out how they came to invest a part of themselves in the places they have inhabited, and how these places have consequently inhabited them. The settings are as quiet as Scott Russell Sanders's small-town Indiana and Stephen Goodwin's Virginia cabin and Anthony Walton's coastal Maine and the Vermont woods that claim Edward Hoagland every spring and summer. And they are as exotic and alive as Ann Beattie's Key West and Anita Desai's Mexico and Madison Smartt Bell's Haiti and Jan Morris's chaotic inner-city Cairo. What all the essays share is the specific connection made in them between internal and external worlds, between the sensibility and art of the essayist and the bricks and mortar that do not feel but are deeply felt.

Place is subjective, of course. Supposing we were to enter the humble wood chapel in Portland that Brian Doyle writes about, enter it through those walnut doors carved intricately with the design of a sunburst. Would we also feel, as he does, something of the infinite in its spaces, feel the mysteries of human existence somehow articulated a little more clearly there? Or if we stepped into the large architectural spaces of the Metropolitan Museum of Art—the Shoin Room, the Temple of Dendur, the Nur al-Din Room—would we feel, as strongly as Phyllis Rose does, not only our sense of time and space pleasantly displaced but also some archetypal part of us connecting with the ancient worlds re-created there? Maybe, maybe not. We respond to places in different ways, after all. But in this regard the great value of the personal essay becomes apparent, for the skilled and visceral essayist can make places we have visited once or twice, or every day, seem altogether different.

Memory plays a vital part in many of these essays, in those gentle pieces by James Conaway, Suzanne Freeman, and John Hough, Jr., for example, depending as they do on the remove of distance and time for perspective and insight. Memory is an elusive, tricky thing. As it traverses time, it can idealize the imperfect, smooth out the bumpy roads, and fetch for us glimpses of the past that seem more comforting than the present. But I am also convinced that a sense of a particular place can be built up in your imagination even if you've never seen it. I have spent most of my life, for example, recklessly faithful to the Chicago Cubs. (Any follower of baseball, no matter how casual, will surely know what great folly there is in such loyalty.) I grew up in southern Illinois, a place as distant in temperament from Chicago as it is in miles. And though the small towns of Little Egypt, as that region is known, are for the most part filled with passionate supporters of the St. Louis Cardinals, I became addicted to the Cubs and to Wrigley Field, their intimate paradise of a ballpark.

For most of my life, I saw the park only on a television screen, but I did so almost every day during baseball season, year upon year. And every day, as a child, I imagined myself in the stands. Without actually being there, but with an imagination that liked to work, I began to *feel* what it was like to sit there on a sunny day, with a stiff wind blowing out to left field, gazing at the ivy on the brick outfield wall and the quaint manually operated scoreboard. All this became as vivid to me, with the passing years, as if I had been going there for ages. A few years ago, I finally visited Wrigley Field for the first time, and though it is a magnificent place, worthy of pilgrimage—charming, elegant, innocent—though the time I spent there was idyllic, I felt some letdown afterward, however slight—and not because the Cubs had lost again. Without my knowing it, the park had taken on its own special life in my mind. How could the actual *place* contend with what I had visualized in my mind's eye, built up over the years, idealized?

I am reminded of the sixth book of Wordsworth's *Prelude,* in which the poet cannot suppress his disappointment upon

seeing Mont Blanc, which he has previously made perfect in
his imagination:

> From a bare ridge we also first beheld
> Unveiled the summit of Mont Blanc, and grieved
> To have a soulless image on the eye
> That had usurped upon a living thought
> That never more could be.

I am not suggesting that the actual Wrigley Field was a soul-
less image on my eye—nothing so harsh as that—but perhaps it was a touch less soulful than the thought of it, which
had lived so vigorously in me until then.

Does the essay, I wonder, possess a similar capacity to dis-
illusion? If the essayist successfully evokes a certain landmark, mythologizes it entirely, is there a danger for the reader
who has never before seen that landmark? In other words,
can the reader's imagination, stimulated by a skillful prose
rendering, devalue the actual physical place, even uninten-
tionally? Perhaps houses and squares and courthouses and
monuments can exist in two ways, occupying both physical
and imaginative realms. But then is it possible to value both
realms equally, or must we necessarily treasure one at the
expense of the other?

What I do know is this: The idea of place roots us, gives us
identity. We are earthbound creatures, and so too are the
things we build, no matter how soaring the skyscraper, how
towering the bridge, how elevating the cathedral. The business of preservation, naturally, is to make sure that things
last. Doesn't our impulse to preserve spring forth from our
very basic affinity with place? If we let the built world fall
apart around us, what would be left of us, the builders?

A
CERTAIN
SOMEWHERE

Paradise Regained

THOMAS MALLON

Flannery O'Connor once complained of "being sawed
in two without ether" when her mother insisted on straight-
ening up the room in which she lived her literary life. Re-
painting was even worse: "It was like the earthquake in
Chile," the novelist wrote in 1960. "It will never be done
again while I live."

Those who live large parts of their imaginative lives in the
Main Reading Room of the New York Public Library made
similar moans during a sixteen-month displacement (July
1997 to November 1998) while the vast octogenarian room
was shut for a $15 million renovation. The whole institution
only managed to function by an unthinkable series of disper-
sals and improvisations. The reference librarians moved
down to the first floor; the Xeroxers, to the south staircase in
Astor Hall. It was a kind of anxiety dream, like being told
someone had decided to rearrange the paintings in the Frick,
the only other New York space that ever seemed unalterable.

For a year and a half one waited through long delays in unfamiliar rooms for the books one absolutely had to have, all
the while wondering just what the renovators were doing up
there on the third floor and whether, when it was over, de-

spite everything they'd promised, you and your fellow refugees might be returning to some horrible new Penn Station for the printed word.

For thirty years, no matter where school or work or travel has taken me, the New York Public Library has been a biblio-Gibraltar, standing through every change in my own fortunes and New York City's. At sixteen, suffering through my first summer job in an office down at Thirty-seventh Street, I would escape each day, four blocks north, to the library's stone steps to eat my lunch. Without enough time to go inside, I would have my sandwich and watch the pedestrians on Fifth Avenue and dream about putting them all into a book that would achieve eternal life in the building behind me—an even grander possibility than having someone read it.

A decade later, in the power-failure summer of 1977, as the city sat in fiscal receivership and lurched into its years of arson and four-digit murder rates, I went as a graduate student to read the personal papers of Georgian poets in the pin-drop silence of the library's Berg Collection. The room that housed it was a good deal more spruce looking than the rest of the building, whose griminess and fatigue, inside and out, made it difficult to believe the library's prospects were any brighter than New York's.

A misapprehension, to be sure. In the twenty years since, the library's slow, steady revival has been the chief harbinger of New York's own recovery. When, in 1981, Vartan Gregorian picked up his new broom (and, in the other hand, a vacuum for philanthropic dollars), the NYPL's patrons got used to seeing stretches of marble coming suddenly clean, old murals being rendered visible, exhibition rooms sporting new paint and gold leaf. Eventually, to the building's immediate west, Bryant Park, filled for years with muggers and syringes, became something more like the Boboli Gardens, sitting atop the library's vast new warren of underground stacks.

The reading room, at the summit of all this rejuvenation, remained more or less untouched. Reassured by everything else going on, I and most other patrons thought that was fine. The plaster ceiling might be flaking and one might occasionally notice glue traps trying to hide themselves from readers and mice, but nothing could seriously detract from the room's gravity-defying grandeur. Look, God, no columns! To receive your requested book, as ever, the only bona fides you had to present was the desire to see it.

By the mid-1980s, possessed of a contract for my work in progress, I was entitled to a key to the Wertheim Study, a ceilingless module squared off by some bookshelves in the reading room's southeast corner. But I never applied for the privilege. The writers in there struck me as aristocrats who'd built themselves a dull little private chapel when right outside it they could have all of Chartres.

The reading room eventually showed up on the pages of some books I researched there. One reviewer of my study of plagiarism took me to task for interrupting a narrative of literary detection to marvel about the place and its procedures. I was describing my search for the Victorian volumes in which I hoped to find one plagiarist's smoking gun:

> One waits for the slips to travel through the pneumatic tubes to the stacks, and then, just minutes later, the pink number matching one's ticket lights up on the board in South Hall, and there, at the counter, are the books: a miracle of ingenuity and municipal munificence, more satisfying than the autoprogrammed cassette that records itself and keeps, like a warm dinner, in the VCR.

The reviewer was right: The wonder of the reading room had got the better of me, and I didn't get back to my story until a whole paragraph had gone by.

Years ago, after being shooshed by a librarian, Holly Golightly (or, at least, Audrey Hepburn) pronounced the reading room not half as nice as Tiffany's, and urged George Peppard to vamoose with her lest the place disrupt their romantic day of exploring New York. To me, though, the room—whose pink-numbered deliveries could be everything you hoped for or terrible disappointments—was as romantic as any place in the city. In my novel *Aurora 7,* it becomes the place where the sex-starved Father Tommy Shanahan declares love to the art history student for whom he's fallen a little earlier in the day. I have him rush up the library steps with some lilies that he's swiped from the altar of St. Agnes's on Forty-third Street. Racing past the guard and into the reading room, he finds the young woman at one of the tables, contemplating a book of Renaissance paintings. He hands her the flowers, which drip water onto the nose of Titian's *Woman at the Mirror.*

And so, just before Christmas, with such a long-standing mental stake in the place, I didn't exactly bound up to the reopened reading room. I approached nervously, pausing at the entrance to notice, straight off, that the two old phone booths (real ones, with seats), behind which lines of impatient callers always formed, were gone. Turning left into South Hall—one of the room's two great halves, split by the book-claim station and its dumbwaiters—I now expected a fusillade of novelty that I was sure to scorn.

My first sensation was of an unfamiliar brightness. New lights shone on the ceiling and bookcases; old blackout paint had been scraped from some of the windows; and all 1,620 bulbs in the eighteen chandeliers appeared—as never before—to be working. The bronze table lamps, all shined up after eighty-seven years, seemed lit from without as well as within.

But all this new illumination soon revealed a space that looked remarkably the same. The little, rarely used lecterns at the edge of some tables were still there, and the tables themselves, gleaming now like their lamps, had been inset with new electrical outlets in the most unobtrusive way imaginable. One would swear the brass-rimmed connections had been there all along, and merely polished up like everything else.

There was, I thought, a different sound. One had heard keystrokes in here for years, but now they made a sort of white-noise waterfall. Sure enough, the computer terminals holding various reference databases have claimed more than a quarter of the tables on South Hall's left side, and new signs urge PLEASE WATCH YOUR WALLETS, PURSES, LAPTOPS, AND OTHER PERSONAL BELONGINGS. And yet there are more seats than there used to be for the unlaptopped and logged off, because the old Wertheim Study has been dismantled and moved down to the second floor.

The great reading room can once more stretch out to its natural length. It's the same in North Hall. The microfilm readers have been permanently banished to another precinct of the library, and the big, featherbedded Xeroxing department has been shrunk into the book-retrieval station between the two halls. (There's also, just in time for the millennium, a spot for self-service copying.) Even with the addition of some handsome information booths, the general feeling is what one gets in the newly restored Grand Central—everything has been cleared of clutter and opened up. Walking along the same old polished terra-cotta tiles, one reaches the edges and ends of the place rather than a lot of blind alleys. At the far-northeast end, I even discover an emergency exit I've never seen before. The two halls have achieved a new sort of parity, since books can henceforth be claimed in both of them—even-numbered call slips in South, odd-numbered in North. The lighted digits announcing the books' arrival now run like a headline ribbon in Times Square.

Pacing the perimeter of both halls, I see all the familiar stretches of books—the green Harvard Classics and the red *Who's Whos*—standing up as though nothing had ever happened. And the inveterates, those readers who've been here day after day for years and years—the dapper, squinting man who looks like a drawing of Voltaire; the fellow with the port-wine mark on his forehead—are all sitting as though nothing had ever happened, as if the sixteen off-limits months had been no more than a sixteen-minute wait for their latest call number to flash. After a while, for all the keystroking, the place even begins to sound the same: When a book is dropped, it still echoes with a great, solemn thud.

Up above, the ceiling ornaments have been repaired and regilded, and the three James Wall Finn paintings, too far gone for restoration, have been replaced by entirely new productions: Yohannes Aynalem's powder-blue skies filled with great pink clouds, three painted rosy dawns over what is now the Rose Main Reading Room, named for the four children of Frederick Phineas Rose and Sandra Priest Rose, donors of the $15 million with which all the work was carried out.

The same quotation from Milton remains inscribed above the great room's doorway:

A Good Booke Is The Precious Life-Blood Of a Master Spirit, Imbalm'd and Treasur'd Up on Purpose To a Life Beyond Life.

Passing back under these lines and going back down the steps, I'm aware of my relief, but I begin to recall something Miltonic that's missing, that's been gone, in fact, for years from its wall space above the next-to-last landing on the north staircase: that enormous painting of the blind poet dictating *Paradise Lost* to his daughters. Where did it ever go?* Even now I can remember the young women looking at Milton with such expectancy, awaiting the words they were about to receive—feeling what I've always felt climbing those stairs.

1999

---

*I've since learned that the painting, done in 1877 by Mihály Munkácsy, now hangs in the library's Edna Barnes Salomon Room, on the third floor.

The Museum of
Who We Were

SUZANNE FREEMAN

LOOKING OUT FROM THE PORCH OF MY GRANDMOTHER'S
house in Murfreesboro, Tennessee, you don't see much—
other small houses with honeysuckle bushes and neat, square
yards; a pale rim of sky; a pair of crooked pine trees; and, on
summer days, a visible shimmer of heat, almost jellylike, just
above the surface of the flat paved road.

By objective standards, it's not a view full of promise or solace. Yet, several years ago, when I needed a home for a displaced child, a grieving and willful and often difficult young
girl, I sent her straight to this spot. I put her directly down on
this porch to consider the stolid, homely landscape and, I
hoped, to learn to be consoled by it. The girl was named Mia,
and the reason I could put her wherever I wanted was that I
invented her. She was the main character in a novel I was trying to write.

I didn't know much about writing a novel, but it seemed
like a good bet to appropriate my grandmother's house for its
setting. Because I did know this place—the one constant of
my own childhood—better than almost anywhere else.

When I was growing up, my family moved often, rarely living in the same house for more than two years. We changed

neighborhoods, schools, states, sometimes even countries. But, from anywhere, you could come back here, open the car door, smell the peculiar, familiar mix of spearmint and gravel dust along the driveway, and—that fast—you would have your bearings. This was the place I counted on for the simple mystery of its being unchanging and true.

My grandmother's house, on East Burton Street, was built in the 1920s of timber logs, stained dark brown and chinked with white mortar, giving it the sort of chocolate-and-vanilla-striped look that you see on old log structures around the Southern countryside. It's something of an anomaly on this street of brick, stone, and stucco dwellings, but it shares the kind of stalwart, almost resolute, stance of its neighbors, which were all built between the world wars.

It reassured us, in summertime, to belong to such a solid place. It taught us much about who we were. The log house was apt to fill up on a July afternoon with uncles and great-aunts and second cousins once removed, sitting in the living room with the shades lowered against the heat, telling family stories, sometimes in dropped voices that made you listen all the harder. This was where I first heard the words *paramour* and *tipsy*. But also *jurisprudence* and *civil rights,* both having to do with members of our own family.

It was a house where we could climb to the attic, sit down on the straw rug in the sweet, stifling air, and read through stacks of Little Lulu or Iodine or Nancy and Sluggo comic books, their pages softened and blurred by light and heat and time. We could play with toys—puppets, soldiers, a marble shooter, a wheezing accordion—that were played with by our fathers, our uncles, and our cousins before. And it was a house filled with photographs of the people we hadn't had a chance to know. Our great-grandfather, the judge, with his full white mustache. Aunt Idalee, her cheeks tinted to a maiden's blush. Our kind-faced grandfather, who woke up one bright morning in this very house, got up from bed, and fell to the floor, dead of a heart attack at age fifty.

In all, this log house was a veritable museum of who we were, and my grandmother found her calling in being its tireless curator. She drew us there, as many of her eleven grandchildren as she could get those summers, and she taught us things—not just the catechism of family but also how to sew on a button and how to peel a peach. She set up a card table in her living room, and we learned to shuffle and deal like card sharks. She taught us slapjack and hearts and crazy eights. At night, we sat out in her big green porch swing, which could hold five or six of us at once, and played parlor games from her own childhood—"the whole stagecoach turned over" or "button-button"—until the dark really settled around us and the house cooled down enough for us to sleep.

Grandma let us drink Coca-Cola, which we weren't allowed to have at home. She bought us packs of Teaberry gum and Cracker Jacks, and each week while we were staying at her house she had a tin of fresh potato chips delivered from the Charles Chips man. She liked spoiling us, but she had certain expectations, too. In her house, we were no longer just citizens of the wide world, we were citizens of her world, where the standards were higher. Here, we had to part our hair straighter and give up nail biting. My grandmother fussed over the clothes we'd brought with us, bleaching our socks whiter, tacking up droopy skirt hems. We had to be on guard against "acting ugly"—telling a lie, for instance, or smacking each other. Anybody who acted ugly was handed a little paring knife and told: "Go on out now and cut a switch."

I don't remember if anybody ever actually got a switching. What I do remember is trudging alone through the steamy backyard with the little knife, considering and rejecting each thin new branch of the peach tree or the mock-orange bush, just imagining its sting. Already, I regretted whatever I'd done. Already, I'd decided I would just be good.

Murfreesboro, set in the exact geographic center of Tennessee, just at the edge of the large shadow cast by Nashville, was growing fast in the early and mid-1960s, those years we spent our summers there. New roads and entire neighborhoods materialized on treeless plots that had recently been cow pastures. The state college became the state university. The population neared twenty thousand. My grandmother didn't bemoan these changes. She liked the bigger stores and the take-out barbecue places. She admired the new houses with their brick patios, their automatic dishwashers. And she could find her way without trouble through the maze of new highway. But to us, it seemed as if she always had some private link with the true heart of the city, with the Murfreesboro where she was born and once knew every family in town.

When our socks were white enough and our fingernails clean enough, she would load us into her 1949 Plymouth and we'd drive down the shady old streets, past my great-aunt's house, down to the town square, dominated by the tall nineteenth-century courthouse where my great-grandfather had served as judge. We'd park the car and go into old stores with dusty floors and ceiling fans that twirled idly overhead. We'd go on to the Murfreesboro Bank, where my grandfather had worked until the day in 1945 he died. In every place, it was the same. A woman would come from behind a counter and greet my grandmother by name. "And who are all these sweet children?" the woman would ask.

My grandmother would turn to look each time, as if astonished at the luck of finding us there, next to her, wearing the shoes she'd recently shined, the skirts she'd hemmed, the faces that took their noses and eyes and shy smiles from the very photographs on her walls.

"Why," she'd say, "these are my grandchildren."

It's not that we ever forgot moments like this, but as we got older and didn't count ourselves among the sweet children any longer, we didn't go back to the log house so often. We meant to, but we didn't. We moved on, in both distance and imagination, to another kind of life—new friends, loud music, summers near a beach. Still, my grandmother never gave up on us. She sent long letters that reached us at summer jobs or college dorms or in foreign countries. They were letters full of simple family stories and weather reports and newspaper clippings, but they carried much more. Somehow, they carried the very essence of a soft Tennessee night spent in a porch swing, pressed arm to sticky arm with cousins, waiting for the thrilling peak of the game when the whole imaginary stagecoach would turn over—and not understanding yet that, in all your life, you would never feel this safe again.

That's why, so many years later, I placed Mia on this porch to start her story. She was a small character in need of someplace safe. So I gave her the porch swing, and I gave her other things I knew about my grandmother's house: the thin slant of sunlight across the kitchen table, the pattern of knotholes in the pine-paneled back bedroom, the dust motes that would fly up if Mia beat her fist against the back of the scratchy red sofa in the living room. I knew the low, steady hum of the refrigerator and the chlorine taste of the water that came from the tap. Just to know these details made the story clearer—and more real—for me. I began to understand what had to happen in the next chapter, and the next. I think it was only because of the log house that I was ever able to get this first book written.

I didn't give Mia everything, though. Her house was in a town called Ionia instead of Murfreesboro. She didn't get any family photographs or the marble shooter or the old comic books. Most important, her house was not built of logs. All of those things belonged to us. I could never just give away what my grandmother had held on to for so long.

And my grandmother did hold on. She held on through a time when her neighborhood changed, when the well-built small houses, long shunned for the new subdivisions, were suddenly popular with young couples again, when people would stop and knock at her door and ask if she'd like to sell her log house.

She held on when she was in her eighties and went outside early one morning to get her newspaper, tripped on her front stepping-stones, and broke her hip. She lay in the chill morning air until it was light enough for somebody to find her and call the ambulance. She went into the hospital for surgery and then into physical therapy, and, defying all the doctors' predictions, she walked and she came home. She held on until the time came, as she had undoubtedly always known it would, when we all came back, more and more often, so that our own children could spend time in the log house. She held her "sweet great-grandbabies." She rocked them in the green porch swing.

My grandmother died in her sleep a few months after her ninety-first birthday. It took another full year before any of us could stand to let the log house go. In that year, I started my novel, already reclaiming the house before it was quite gone. I don't think I would have dreamed of setting pesky Mia down on that porch while my grandmother was alive. Mia acted ugly. My grandmother would have sized her right up and sent her out to cut a switch. End of story.

The last time I went to the house was just before it was sold, a scorching-hot June day. We all arrived from Massachusetts and North Carolina and Ohio with rental trucks and vans. We took down the photographs, and we divided the furniture and all the other things. Somehow, I was too late for the marble shooter, but I got my grandmother's button box, which we'd used for those games of button-button. I can think now of how we sat night after night in a row on the porch swing, hands cupped in front of us, while my grandmother, standing, moved from child to child, ready to slip a thin bone button into one lucky pair of hands.

"Hold fast what I give you," she would say to each of us, touching her hands to ours. "Hold fast what I give you."

1997

The Peaceable Kingdom

EDWARD HOAGLAND

I T'S TOO GOOD TO BE TRUE, I'VE ALWAYS THOUGHT, FOR THE past twenty-eight years, when spring rolls around once again and I drive up to my warm-weather home, now the only occupied house on a four-mile stretch of dirt road that crosses a mountain notch in northeastern Vermont: a two-story frame dwelling, painted blue-gray and nearly a hundred years old, built by the first family who cleared these sparse fields. They had forty acres, ten or twelve cows, and three other families for neighbors, two living in log cabins that have since fallen in—enough kids for a one-room school, which later was moved next door, when that family's original house burned and they needed a new one. My predecessors had thrown together a log cabin at first; a barge-shaped depression in the woods still marks where it was. Then, when they decided to stay, they dug a cellar hole here with a horse-drawn scoop, split some granite boulders at the base of the cliff for blocks of stone to line it with, and set up a sawmill to cut floorboards of spruce. Sand from the stream was used for the plastering, and they planted apple trees and a black cherry tree and four oaks, now nice and big, in front.

The farming ceased about forty years ago. The man I

bought the house from was supporting himself by brewing corn whiskey and bathtub beer and shooting deer out of season for meat. He died too soon from drinking too much, and his British war-bride wife afterward, though she was a favorite person of mine and planted many of the flower beds I continue to enjoy. The lack of electric and phone lines had made them eager to move, and indeed explains why this mountain road has never been as unpopulated as it is now and why beyond my house it is being abandoned "to the Indians," as the town authorities say.

What I do when I arrive is air and sweep the house, load the woodstove, turn the water on, browse my bookshelves for a glimpse of old friends, and check to see if the local ermine spent the winter inside clearing the place of the few pairs of white-footed mice that otherwise might have chewed my socks. Thus, I prefer to find her hairy little twists of dung over anybody else's. Chipmunks, when they wake from semi-hibernation, may seek entry also.

I open the four bird boxes that hang on trees to clear out squirrel nests—if any red squirrels had sheltered there through the snowy months—hoping that now tree swallows will come instead. I climb into the hayloft of the barn to see if a bear slept out the season in the mounds of hay, or merely some raccoons, and look, too, for the phoebes, early arrivals that nest under my eaves, then listen for white-throated sparrows, ovenbirds, yellowthroats, wood thrushes, robins, winter wrens, rose-breasted grosbeaks, chestnut-sided warblers, mourning warblers, and black-throated green, and black-throated blue, and black-and-white warblers. Cedar waxwings, indigo buntings, flickers, and goldfinches will be arriving. A certain apple-tree limb is where the hummingbirds will nest.

If the large mother coon has survived the winter, she will probably be using the hollow maple as a den tree. By putting my ear next to it, I may hear her kits. The ermine (now an ordinary brown weasel) that protected my woolens has meanwhile moved from the house to nest among the timbers of the barn. Investigating clues perhaps left by the bear in the hayloft, I'll hear her burbling expressions of alarm. The mother woodchuck hibernates under the chicken coop and reappears as soon as the grass does; and if I'm lucky, I'll see a migrating trio of black ducks sneak in at dusk for a night's rest—out of the hurly-burly of the lakes nearby—in my high-up, hidden frog pond. They'll eat some water greens at dawn and then be gone. Bears will have already clipped off the young spring sedges at water level. Sedges are among the first foods bears taste; or they trudge to the fir woods a few hundred yards downhill, where some deer have generally wintered, to find out if any died. I look for antlers the living bucks have dropped, but bears sniff for a carcass they can eat, though they will gobble deer droppings, too, in this hungry time, and search for last fall's sprouted beechnuts on the ground.

The lawn under my oaks, mossy and mushroomy, doesn't need much mowing. The apple trees mainly feed the wildlife, and I Bush Hog the fields only often enough to keep them open. The stream was dammed seventy-five years ago for homegrown experiments with water power but flows just as it wishes now, and moose, deer, and coyotes drink from it instead of cows. I sometimes do, too, or kingfishers, ravens, or woodcock make use of it, and a great blue heron hunts mice and frogs alongside. I had the frog pond dug, hiring a bulldozer for the purpose of filling the air with song. Spring peepers and wood frogs start up in April. Then tree frogs, green frogs, pickerel frogs, and of course toads—my favorite serenaders of all—join in. As the lush orchard grass and the thick raspberry patch sloping away from the old barn have lost their soil nutrients from half a century's worth of cow manure from the animals that were stabled there, fireweed and other hardscrabble plants replaced them and what had been a teeming colony of earthworms became scarcer. This was tough on the family of garter snakes living underneath my house, which had fed on them. But the frogs, increasing tenfold, took up some of the slack as a food source.

These garter snakes, just twenty miles short of Canada, are blacker than the same species in southern Vermont, because they need to absorb as much heat as possible during the brief summer season in order to digest what they eat; the sun is their engine. The woodchucks are blacker, too, not to accumulate heat but as camouflage: In these northern forests, dark fur shows up less. The bears are black, the moose are black, the porcupines dark. The deer in their red summer coats look quite odd, as in fact they should, because they followed the white men north.

In the house, I load the flashlights, put candles around, fill the kerosene lamps, and look to see if anything has been pilfered over the winter—pipe wrenches, a fire extinguisher, boots, blankets, or possibly my ax? Secondhand books sell hereabouts for a dollar a box, so no one steals books, though somebody once purloined the magnifying glass that went with my *Oxford English Dictionary*. And, once, my field glasses were lifted, just before hunting season started, yet then were left on my woodpile during December. The next year, when it happened again, they weren't returned—this being such an impoverished area that woodpiles, too, are sometimes stolen. A furniture factory is the principal local employer, using the yellow birch and rock maple that people log around here when they aren't cutting pulpwood. Unemployment is so high it keeps wages low. Some people truck milk to Massachusetts, or cattle to the hamburger slaughterhouses down there. Where you see goshawks, red-tailed and broad-winged hawks, and peregrine falcons, you don't notice ads in the paper saying HELP WANTED.

My windows and rooms are small, as befits the cold climate most of the year. On some of the richest days, when a moose stalks by or a bear is blueberrying or munching hazelnuts outside, I think of my house as a bathysphere suspended in the wilderness. Nevertheless, it's comfortable—the floors painted russet, the furniture homey, the walls nearly covered with pictures I've taped up over the last quarter-century. I'm partly surrounded by an eight-thousand-acre state forest, to which I'm leaving my land as a minor addition, except for the house, which will belong to my daughter. Big Valley Brook, Stillwater Swamp, May Pond, Boiling Spring, and Moose Mountain are spectacles that live in my head, yet I can walk to. If the weather muscles in, I chop four hours' worth of wood. I hear an owl; I hear the ravens; I hear a redstart.

GARDENERS AND TROUT fishermen got busy outdoors around mid-April, if the high water permitted, and the kids in town started shagging fungoes or fishing Kids' Brook, a stretch of stream near the fairgrounds so easy that it's lent to them. For me, spring had begun a month earlier, when a big male bobcat's tracks looped down off Moose Mountain into my wooded notch and intersected in a romancing scrawl with the solitary lady bobcat who shares the area with me. When the snow is gone, her movements become more of a mystery, of course, but my dog has treed her. On other rare occasions, I notice her prints beside the pond or hear a rabbit scream at night, utterly suddenly, caught from ambush.

Then on the last day of March a bear that dens near my house left her little cave to enjoy what was perhaps her first drink in four months. Going a hundred feet so she could lap the trickling meltwater in a brook, her tracks showed that she made an immediate return trip to sleep some more. On Tax Day she was still in her den, her head protruding dozily, but the next day she descended a quarter-mile to a patch of swamp to eat some cattails, with yearling-size tracks accompanying her. The presence of the grown cub meant that, in the bearish biennial ritual, a male would probably come visit us in June so she could have new cubs next winter.

Among certain Indian tribes, a family used to inherit a given cluster of bear dens, along with the winter nutrition to be gained by killing the occupants in prudent rotation. Though I avail myself of the local supermarket, I'm just as protective: Don't mess with my bears. And the dog doesn't. Wally is a sheepdog and patrols the meadow aggressively but regards the forest as foreign territory. On the other hand, when the county airstrip comes to life and low-flying Cessnas angle over, he is inspired to defend the perimeter of our empty field from these roaring eagles with a pell-mell frenzy, as if we had a bevy of lambs that they might grab. Then after chasing a plane away, he'll cock his leg and pee triumphantly against a tree, the same as when his adversary has been a wandering fox or coyote, so it will know next time who it must reckon with.

He'll also mark a rabbit's trail, a squirrel's roost, a mouse's nest for later reference when he hunts, although I doubt he is one tenth as efficient at that occupation as a fox. In June, I'll lie in the field at dusk and listen to a vixen's hectic rustle as she gleans a stomachful of meadow mice, deer mice, shrews, moles, night crawlers, and such to take back to her burrow and vomit for her pups. And I remember how quickly a woodchuck that had grown feisty from taunting Wally at the mouth of its hole fell prey to a lank coyote that rambled through. The coyote carried the body off, but stopped, dropped it, and performed an unexpected sort of victory dance, stiff-legged, around the corpse.

Joy walking is what deer hunters call what I do in the woods, because I bring no gun. For Wally as well, our outings are a matter of glee, not necessity. He'd rather simply haul home a dehorned head or a gut pile that a poacher has left than hunt for more than a few minutes himself. Carrion tastes, I suspect, a bit winy, cheesy, anchovy-and-green-olivey, béarnaise-and-sour-creamy (which may be why we late primates try so hard to approximate the piquancy of fermentation with sauces). Wally drinks from muddy puddles and nibbles green sprouts as a further change from piped-in water and dog kibble before curling at my head as a sentinel when we camp out.

Wally celebrated spring around Tax Day by running down to the pond alone for his first swim: this when the wood frogs and song sparrows had just started to sing. I was lolling in a patch of sunny grass, watching a pair of robins, listening to a kinglet and a phoebe but, lest my delight seem unadulterated, also picking off my first tick of the season. Instead of forest lore, Wally has become adept at reading human beings (hunters are the only predators he flees), such as the precise moment every morning when he can jump on my bed without waking and angering me—or the extraordinary value I place on the welfare of the goofy parrot in the kitchen versus the crows in the garden, which he is encouraged to chase. They fly up into the basswood tree and razz him, then look for a hawk they can mob and mistreat.

1997

Hiding Out in
Mañanaland

ANN BEATTIE

K EY WEST . . . SOUTHERNMOST POINT IN THE CONTI-
nental United States; ninety miles from Cuba; the (as Rickie
Lee Jones might say) Last Chance Texaco of the Florida Keys.
It's the hot place to set your mystery novel, the place to go on
spring break if you can shine through in a wet T-shirt contest,
a perfect place to protest self-righteously if you don't believe
that cats in clown collars should spend their evenings jump-
ing through burning hoops. There's residential Key West and
then there's the tourist town, but wherever you are, the traffic lets you know it's no sleepy-time sort of place. Like parts
of New Orleans, it's one of those cities where houses sit close
to the sidewalk or on small plots of land. People tend not to
pull the shades—in fact, they don't necessarily have them—
and front doors are often thrown open, making life inside
quite visible to passersby. The action, though, tends to be
behind the house, where doors open onto private gardens,
some with enormous trees, some with gurgling fishponds
(often covered in netting so cranes won't get the expensive
fish), all with tropical flowers.

The gardens go some way toward explaining Key West:
This is a place of hidden places; it's filled with hidden cor-

ners, where many things are done in secret. As you might expect, these things are not necessarily legal. There are wonderful, tiny alleys, along which people manage further privacy for their already obscure homes by erecting very high fences. There is a private plot called the Secret Garden, a sort of faux–tropical rain forest that visitors search for, often inconclusively: down a lane, behind a fence, drop your money in a jar (in this way, it does not resemble a tropical forest).

Movie stars can find privacy in Key West, assuming they want it; Salman Rushdie showed up mid–book tour for dinner last winter. For a while, there was something called "celebrity watch" on the local radio. One day there was a sighting of the Beaver (a.k.a. Jerry Mathers) selling hot dogs, or whatever it was, down by Smathers Beach. But the next day the Beaver had pulled up stakes—this is the sort of thing you come to expect in Key West—and the local radio station was on to the next celeb.

Key West is not a tranquil haven; its parameters are small, and the craziness from the main drag, Duval Street, spills over into Old Town, where handsome Victorian houses are in a constant state of repair and renewal. A quintessential Key West image is this: a largely unclothed house owner, in stunning physical shape, standing around by his Jeep, which is parked on the curb (that's right; the streets are narrow), talking on a cellular phone while his house is being demolished by crews who work as quickly and effectively as tropical termites. Like the rest of our nation, Key West is under construction, though the workmen—to say nothing of the owners—are not what you'd expect from central casting. My husband and I once rented a house with a garden that was tended by an intimidatingly large motorcycle-macho-man clad in black leather and many decorative chains, whom we later saw performing at a poetry slam. It's a place where you have your day job and then you have your other job—or, equally likely, it's a place where you have no job at all.

It is essential to know this about Key West: Much of the day is spent in preparation for evening, and for night. If by mid-afternoon you stop drinking Cuban espresso shots that make your ears burn, the caffeine will gradually work its way out of your system in time for early-evening Jell-O shots that will soothe your tired throat and prepare you for a night of continued drinking. Tie-dyed clothes that look a bit tacky in full sun take on a mellow glow as the sun begins to sink. And just before sunset there is the nightly celebration at Mallory Square, much advertised in guidebooks, which try valiantly to make it sound like fun. Here, latter-day Houdinis say politically reprehensible things about the role of women in men's lives in order to get laughs as they struggle to escape their triple-locked chains, and the self-named Cookie Lady pedals around on her bike, announcing her homemade confections with a voice that brings to mind Maria Callas during pesky arguments with Onassis. Then the aforementioned kitty cat makes the big jump. After the trainer passes the hat (not on fire), he can use the proceeds to buy kitty his nightly tuna fish.

Key West is not the place it was, everyone who's been around a while will tell you emphatically. It's become crowded and noisy, dirty and increasingly dangerous. If you've got a source at the hospital, you can find out how many spring-breakers really wipe out on motorcycles and those silly pink motor scooters they rent. But you shouldn't romanticize the good old days too much. Yeah, it was fun, those years of grossing out the ladies by tossing down tequila from a bottle with a worm sunk in it, and deep-sea fishing and diving and dancing—there's not one decent dance place left to take your slave anymore. But back in the bad old days, the pirates were not gentlemanly, and Audubon himself, whose house you may tour, carried out his own mini–My Lai by blasting away birds. The Hemingway house, *si!* But even Papa was a sort of pirate, complete with bad leg, though he tended to round up women instead of shipboard treasures.

Key West has always been slightly glamorous, but along with the glamour has come a jaded, faded beauty, as well as an implicit message that one would do well to acquire a bit of ironic detachment about the place, as well as about one-self. I mean, who really calls any place paradise, circa 1997? What do you make of a place where the mayor once water-skied to Cuba? What do you say about room-service menus whose breakfast offerings begin with a page of tropically in-spired alcoholic beverages? This sprightly place briefly se-ceded from the United States to declare itself the Conch Republic. Better not to be shocked. Better to go with the flow. During the winter, enough gray-suit guys who've de-cided to step out still put in an appearance in cutoffs, strange hats with brims shaped like pelican beaks or with foam-rubber breasts above the brim, and Birkenstocks (preferably worn with acid-green-and-pink argyles) that you'll never fail to be amused on a day's outing. These days full drag is rare, but someone with the je ne sais quoi to wear the same collar as his pet porcupine is still entertaining. If we can't have Fan-tasy Fest—an official parade, almost a quaint throwback to American customs elsewhere—every day, at least don't deny anyone the little sporadic homages. A few feathers always make a person merrier.

Paradoxically, Key West is about lying low and also about being noticed. A bunch of writers cluster here in the winter and, amazingly, there is no grandstanding, no envy or malice.

You could argue that the place is so small that for the sake of sanity everybody has got to get along, though that theory doesn't seem to work very well with jails. No: The goodwill in Key West is sincere. I suppose the climate helps one's general disposition, as does the shared sense that everyone is getting away with something.

Real world? A place where you have implicit or explicit dress codes? Where animals are not necessarily welcome, no matter how nicely dressed? Awakening to an alarm clock instead of to a rooster? Shoveling snow instead of strolling over to one of the big hotels and smirking at a blackboard on the beach that lists the frigid temperatures elsewhere in the nation? Surely this congested and crazy Margaritaville-as-Mañanaland is the sort of place to take a vacation but not to live and work, right?

To tell you the truth, I don't think so. It's easy for me not to think so, because nobody wants to hire my husband or me anyway. We've been out of the workaday-world loop for so long—he's a painter; I'm a writer—that in spite of envious people who'd like to put that loop around our necks and pull hard, the idea of having a more regular life just doesn't apply. It also doesn't agree with a lot of people from our generation, the two of us included. We're antsy. We want quick fixes and—no different from certain Romantic poets—long periods in which to consider what we've seen and done. We're short-tempered, alternately solitary and sociable, maladjusted, and we both have few delusions about fitting in. But while I consider us lucky, I don't consider us unique. I don't think we're the only people improvising lives or molting with the seasons. In middle age, I'm seeing more and more people of my generation slithering out from under the heap of benefits + boredom that was once called job security. People are choosing to pursue their hobbies rather than their vocations. They're taking early retirement. They're ready to slip down the rabbit hole into places that make comfortable repositories for the dislocated—such as Key West.

I think there are a lot of marginal people out there from my generation, and I don't think that *marginal* is necessarily a pejorative term. We don't define ourselves in terms of our family identity—Mommy and Daddy often have different last names—and we've changed jobs, if not careers, so often we certainly don't define ourselves in terms of corporate loyalties. People who can't land a job—or, more likely, who can't bear to make the concessions necessary to keep one—have suddenly cast themselves as glamorous wild cards: They're "consultants." If they occasionally work at something, they're "freelancers." They don't go to the office; they go to the home office. (The whole concept of *office* is distressing to me. I refer to the room I work in as *the bedroom*—which it was, when somebody else owned our house. Even then, I often move my modem-less computer from my fax-less room and plug it in on the back porch so I can use the picnic table. I, too, have the delusion of freedom.)

Since so many of us always had a real distrust of big corporations, what kind of a reflection on us has it been that we couldn't get along so brilliantly in them? For a while in the eighties we were conditioned to think primarily about money. Then revisionism set in, and we were given the message to forget about money. Newthink: primarily about family. Family grown, dispersed: Whoa! What was that all about?, and once more into the fray, this time with a new set of expectations. We were already expanding dress-down Fridays into Fridays that didn't even exist as workdays. Those looong weekends became an opportunity to travel, but short-term travel was just stealing bases, the weekend trips to the Hamptons just sprinting to train for the big race. Once we'd bought L. L. Bean replacements for our old safari jackets, it was off to Nepal. India. Provence. All the places the nomads and malcontents who've made rootlessness into a career, and all the places the writers going from the desperate academy to the desperate city to the desperate country have been telling us we must check out.

Though, for the long term, those places have proved to be just so far away. Here's my solution: Find within America a place that seems not very much like America. If you squint (easy, in the sun, to say nothing of those "special" margaritas), Key West can seem like a foreign country. At the very least, you can mistake it for some place in the Caribbean. It's a tropical island where they (sort of) speak your language. And it's got it all: charm and corruption, natural beauty and highway sprawl, disgruntled activists as well as the disfranchised. It's definitely not the cutting edge—it's more like the remnant that got snipped. But there it is: oddly configured, perhaps useful, for those good at improvising. I'd be willing to bet that if Jay Gatsby were just appearing on the scene, he might well summer on Long Island, but he'd winter in Key West. I can see him in the doorway of his big, renovated house, probably in the new, trendy neighborhood of big houses, near the Casa Marina. There he'd be, dressed in his pink shirt, expecting an odd, flamboyant assortment of company, ever the gentleman, but determined to get back something very important he'd lost. Convinced that how you appeared, and how you lived, coupled with the sheer force of your desire, must bring it to you.

1997

Doorway to Heaven

BRIAN DOYLE

PIETRO BELLUSCHI BUILT IT, USING WOODS OF THE PACIFIC Northwest—yellow fir for the beams, hemlock and pine for the roof, white oak for the floor, Sitka spruce for the balcony, silver maple for the sills, cherry for the walls, altar, chairs, kneelers, and lectern. Behind it are muscular oaks and madroña trees and tall, lean Douglas firs as straight as poles, and adjacent is a thicket of laurels and rhododendrons so old that their arms are thicker than your legs. Here Belluschi wanted to make a holy cabin that would fit its place, a chapel for the University of Portland big enough for hundreds of people and thousands of prayers but not so big that it would be arrogant—not here, not against those massive oaks, the immense Willamette River, the forest that once housed the biggest trees in the history of the world.

He used brick and stone and tile, too, the stones drawn from local rivers and arranged as a little streambed outside the chapel to course away the rain from its gutterless tile roof. He wanted mammoth doors, herculean doors, doors as big as dories, so he asked his friend Leroy Setziol to carve them, which he did, and the posts and lintels, too, huge things, big as trees.

Setziol had been in the Second World War and had hidden in caves from Japanese snipers on remote islands in the Pacific. An ordained minister, he came home to Maryland after the war, but when he welcomed black people into his congregation, he was invited to not be a minister anymore, and eventually he ended up in Oregon, where he decided to become a wood carver, although he had never picked up a gouge or chisel in his life. It turned out that he was a sort of genius at carving wood. "Wood is the history of its own living," he says. "I try to cooperate with it, and feel for unknown properties and unpredictable events. That's about as well as I can explain it."

Setziol waited and waited for the right wood to cooperate with, and one day three huge black walnut trees washed up on the Oregon coast, and he had them hauled to his wood shop in the hills near the old timber town of Willamina, and there he cut the doors and lintels, four tons of walnut incised with a sunburst, and a branching vine, and Greek letters, and other signs and symbols of Christ.

Belluschi found an ancient ivory crucifix for the tiny side chapel where the faithful are shriven of their sins, and a glassmaker to make the densely colored inch-thick stained-glass windows, and a priest who was a scholar of ancient Christian baptisteries to design the concrete baptismal fountain that trickles all night and day like a creek running through the nave of the chapel, and a massive organ from Austria, and a thick tapestry from the Netherlands, and then the chapel was finished just as summer closed up shop fourteen years ago.

It was dedicated in early October, on a bright, windy day. Priests, donors, and students spoke, and then Belluschi spoke, briefly, fingering a scrap of paper on which he had jotted notes.

"A church is much more than a building," he said. "It is people coming together to evoke God's harmony. It is our hope that the qualities which we have tried to impart to this structure, inadequate as they may be, will endure, and move people to incomparable adventures of the spirit."

When he sat down he crammed the scrap of paper back into his jacket pocket, but a sharp-eyed priest later asked him for it, and the university for which Pietro Belluschi built his little wooden chapel still has a copy of the paper, now carefully framed and hanging in its museum.

A FRIEND OF mine died while climbing a mountain. He was a professor of physics, a baseball player, a lover of women, a fly fisherman, a student of astronomy, a man with a car in which he kept clothes, books, coffee cups, cleats, student papers, beer bottles, boots of various sorts, a gyroscope, reels, and the front wheel of a bicycle. A thousand tons of ice fell on him, and he died. He was the last man in a line of thirteen men and women climbing Mount Hood late in the afternoon of a sunny day in May. He volunteered to be last so he could help with any trouble above him. An avalanche missed the first twelve climbers and caught Tom. This was on a Sunday. The next Friday there was a ceremony in the chapel. The chapel had seen funerals before, oh yes, plenty of funerals, but this latest tragedy was a raw wound, a young man crushed on the mountain that gleamed coldly behind the chapel, and it wasn't a funeral exactly. It was a remembering, and it was different.

People stared at the mountain for a long time as they walked up to the chapel.

The doors were flung open and the side door was propped open and the back door was propped open, too, and the wind sifted through, shuddering the candles—a west wind carrying a whiff of cedar from the huge forest across the river.

Tom had been a headlong man, furious and passionate and merciful and disorganized, which breeds great affection. His friends were alive with stories of him. He had forgotten this and that, shouted and courted at the wrong times, wandered the world. His mind was a silver machine, and his house and car and office were monuments to chaos. He once ran out to left field in a baseball game wearing fishing waders, having driven furiously from a river to the ballpark without bothering to change. He asked of his students "ragamuffin irreverence for wisdom," as he said. He asked to teach a university course in astronomy because he knew nothing about it and wished to know a great deal about it. He kept a class out all night counting meteor showers. He took a class snowshoeing in April on the mountain that would kill him.

A priest stood and said that he had not slept for days after Tom died and did not know what he would possibly be able to say at this event when suddenly one night the psalms came to him, whole singing snatches of them, and he rose from his useless bed and opened a Bible and found Psalm 24: "The man whose heart is pure will climb the mountain of the Lord. . . . The Lord's is the earth and its fullness, the world and all its peoples. Who shall climb the mountain of the Lord? Who shall stand in his holy place? The man with clean hands, who desires not worthless things, who has not sworn so as to deceive his neighbor. . . . Such are the men who seek the face of God."

Those words rang around the wooden chapel, and I watched as hands went to mouths, hands covered eyes, hands rose suddenly, hands folded into prayer wings. The arcs traced by hands describing infinite emotions, hands as the hawks of the heart.

Hours after the remembering was done, I went back to sit vigil and noticed that the doors were still open, and slicing through the chapel in glee and confusion were dozens of swallows, barn swallows and tree swallows, their bright bellies flashing in the russet light as they wheeled over the baptistery, altar, organ, and balcony, up into the little turret at the top of the building and back down with zooming swoops, in and out of the chapel in numbers I could not count, although I tried, feeling it important to number the feathers on the heads of even the smallest of the quicksilver visitors that day. But there was more life there than I could measure.

IT'S ONE LARGE wooden room, essentially, which provides much of its delight; a vaulting cathedral is a lovely and heroic thing, but such a spiritual battleship is designed for awe and humility, not intimacy, and in my middle years I believe that the small is far more likely to bear the fingerprints of the Incomprehensible than the vast. So I study small and quiet things: children, insects, the grace of old women shuffling to impatient buses. And I sit in this one small chapel, drawn to it not so much for its role as religious house, although I have an abiding respect and affection for Catholicism, but for its virtues as prism, refuge, fulcrum; it is a room where powers and pains of all sorts are gathered again and again and again, simmered and melded and melted and stewed. Perhaps that daily marshaling of emotion is what gives the place its holiness, more than its official duties do. Perhaps words and smoke and tears and music and long, empty hours all soak into the wooden walls and season them in unimaginable ways.

The chapel is not all dignity and grace, of course; there are three small offices in it, and often I have heard a phone ringing angrily during mass—once, incredibly, just as the priest was hoisting the consecrated Host aloft, the very moment when Catholics believe a miracle of transformation occurs. An elevator groans its way to the balcony aloft, the tapestry behind the altar is pious pap, the organ squats hugely and toadishly out of proportion with the clean, simple wooden lines of the rest of the place, and one or two of the lights overhead are always burned out.

Yet somehow its flaws warm it. No building can be intimidating if its elevator growls like a crusty uncle and its brassy telephones snarl with no respect at all for the rituals, as old as human civilization, enacted there. I have loved and savored chapels and churches and prayer rooms and temples around the world, but something about this wooden room continues to captivate me. I have seen people married here, and dead men waked, and infants baptized, and robed teenagers welcomed into the church, and I have seen people prostrate in prayer in the dark, their arms flung out on the floor like fingered wings. I have seen weeping and fainting and laughing and dancing. I have seen a blind priest conduct a mass. I have seen two young, strong, pliant boys carry their broken father to the altar for a blessing. I have seen a long line of people folding themselves down to the floor to kiss a rough wooden cross on Good Friday, the darkest day of the Catholic year, when Catholics touch the sign of the thin, gaunt man they believe broke time into Before and After. I have chanted poetry there, the songs of William Blake, and I have heard music there to shred your heart, and I have heard a priest sing a mass there from beginning to end, a thing hardly done in the world now, a riveting thing.

I have seen people there at dawn and at dusk, at noon and in the blue hours of the night. Once, I croaked open the walnut doors long after midnight and saw a man kneeling and weeping, and I turned and left, the chapel suddenly too small for more than one penitent.

There are as many places to pray as there are manners of praying, but some places have a peculiar power and poetry that make them conducive to contemplation, amenable to a shiver in the soul. Great waters incline me to prayer; and so does midnight, when my wife and children are asleep and I cover them with blankets and stare at their sculpted faces; and so do lanky, leggy herons for some reason; and so does the cedar chapel Belluschi built, the room made of wood in the woods, a house for incomparable adventures of the spirit.

2001

Rooms to Grow In

MORRIS HALLE

AN ARTICLE THAT I READ SOME TIME AGO QUOTED AN
architect to the effect that every new building is like a jail.
Once a building is up, he said, the people for whom it was
built have to stay in it. Escape is difficult; in most cases, impossible.

The architect didn't describe the situation correctly: Inhabitants of a building think of escape and jails only when the
building does not fit their needs and life inside becomes hard
to bear. To my mind, buildings are rather like shoes: One
thinks of changing shoes or of not wearing shoes at all mainly
when they don't fit. When the shoes fit, we wear them without conscious thought and would not dream of being without
them.

These thoughts occurred to me as I was considering the
building in which I had an office during my entire teaching
career (1951–1996) at the Massachusetts Institute of Technology. The building, at 18 Vassar Street in Cambridge, was
erected in 1943 as a temporary home of the Radiation Laboratory, charged with development of aircraft radar and other
electronic devices important to the conduct of World War
Two. Similar temporary structures were erected all over the

country, but almost all were taken down soon after the fighting ended. Our building, known in MIT nomenclature as Building 20, remained in constant use for more than half a century after the war.

It was very horizontal: 250,000 square feet in a long, three-story, flat-roofed block sprouting four parallel wings from one side. MIT graduate Don Whiston designed the building in an afternoon, and it was readied for occupancy in six months. All steel was committed to the war, so Building 20 was framed with heavy wood timbers (which required an exemption from the city's fire code), and it was covered with asbestos shingles. It's been called funky, nerdy, and plain ugly, but Building 20 fit many of us perfectly. The basic room module was large, twelve by twenty-four feet, with asbestos walls and an acoustic-tile ceiling. Exposed pipes and wires ran overhead the length of the corridors. When the layout of an office or laboratory had to be changed, the alteration could be done at little expense and with a minimum of disturbance to the neighbors.

The building kept us dry and warm in winter except on those rare occasions when a window fell out because it had never been reputtied. Most of us in Building 20 were also comfortable in summer, because the windows were so simply constructed that installing a room air conditioner was completely straightforward, at least most of the time. I recall one occasion when an installation did not go altogether smoothly, but since we were in Building 20, the matter was quickly fixed. In about 1967 my office mate, linguist Noam Chomsky, and I decided that the summer was unbearably hot and that we needed to air-condition our office. As we had no budget for this extravagance, we decided to pay for it ourselves, and ordered two air conditioners from a department store. Some-

time after the units were up and running and we were enjoy-
ing their effects, I received a call informing me that we had
failed to obtain a permit for installing the air conditioners. My
caller identified himself as a representative of a committee
charged with safeguarding the architectural outlines of the
buildings at MIT. I pointed out that we were talking about
Building 20 and added that I was not about to do anything
about our air conditioners. We hung up, and I never heard
about the matter again.

Not everybody liked Building 20. I remember interviewing
a secretary for possible employment in our group. At the end
of the interview she said that the building was so unappeal-
ing, so deadening to the soul, that accepting our offer—even
if one were to be forthcoming—was out of the question. And
Chomsky has had occasional visitors who asked him whether
he had another office and expressed surprise when the answer was no.

The greatest virtue of Building 20 was that during most of
its existence, space in it was not at a premium and did not
have to be fought over in the way space is fought over in
really desirable campus locations. Of all the blessings that
came to us from occupying Building 20, I consider this the
most important. I estimate that it added five years to my
scholarly life, years that would have been spent fighting for
space. Moreover, because it was a relatively undesirable site,
Building 20 could perform its most important function, that of
incubator for new developments. We know that research is
risky, that new ideas often are wrong. But without trying
them out, one cannot tell the few good ideas from the many
that are less good. To find out, one needs not only money but
also space. No one at MIT keeps records of such matters, so
we do not know how many deserving projects stalled at the

talking stage because there was no space for them. But we do know that because there was space in Building 20, many quite risky projects got off the ground. Innovative laboratories for the study of nuclear science, cosmic rays, dynamic analysis and control, and food technology incubated in Building 20. Among the many successful projects that found a home there were the important experiments by Jerome Y. Lettvin on the physiology of vision and audition of the frog; Jerrold Zacharias's work on the atomic clock; and Harold Edgerton's studies on stroboscopic photography.

Of course, not every project housed in Building 20 was successful. For example, around 1950 the great Norbert Wiener (1894–1964), the father of cybernetics and one of the leading mathematicians of his generation, conceived that humans could learn to perceive speech if the signal was filtered into a number of frequency bands and transmitted to different spots on their bodies, say, to the fingertips. (Wiener, I believe, got the idea from Aldous Huxley's *Brave New World,* where in addition to movies there were spectacles known as feelies.) The idea did not fly, and I know about it only because in 1951 I shared 20B-201—that is, Room 201 in Wing B of Building 20—with a graduate student who was trying to put Wiener's idea into practice.

Linguistics, my own field of specialization, was one of those high-risk projects that but for the existence of Building 20 would not have developed at MIT. The availability of space had an enormous influence on the way the linguistics program evolved not only at MIT but worldwide. Linguistics has been part of the humanities or liberal arts since the Middle Ages, when grammar, rhetoric, and logic formed the trivium, the set of studies required of all who would obtain the bachelor's degree. Study in the humanities has traditionally involved much reading and thinking and relatively little doing. A library reading room is typically where students do much of their work, and conversation there is discouraged, if not altogether prohibited. As a consequence, students in the humanities often conduct their thesis research in isolation from their peers and colleagues.

This approach is very different from the way advanced study is conducted in the sciences and engineering. In these fields, the main site of activity is the often noisy laboratory, where there are a great many people working on related problems. Some of them are students; others may be faculty members, visitors, or researchers employed at the laboratory. In such a setting, learning frequently results from interactions with others. Characteristically, new students in a laboratory are taught much of what they need to know by their colleagues, and the teaching is largely informal.

By a fortunate coincidence, I was exposed to this type of learning when I first came to MIT in 1951 as an assistant professor. I did not have a Ph.D., and the biggest attraction of the job was that it provided an opportunity for doing research on speech, which I could then use for my Ph.D. thesis at Harvard. I was given a bench in 20B-201, which I shared with that graduate student, whose field was electrical engineering, but who was also interested in speech. The student had set up some equipment to measure various acoustic properties of speech. I did not know the first thing about this equipment, nor did I have much of an understanding of the acoustics of speech. But my laboratory mate and others in Building 20 turned out to be excellent teachers, from whom I was able to learn a great deal, especially since somebody always seemed to be available to answer questions or carry on discussions. I soon learned enough to begin research of my own and to collaborate with others, who were working on related problems. One of the people with whom I collaborated was Ken Stevens, a chaired professor of electrical engineering. We coauthored our first paper in 1959, and the ninth in this series, which we hope is not the last, should be completed later this year.

In the 1950s, there were a number of other research projects in Building 20 that employed linguistics. The biggest of these was a project on machine translation, which, as its name implies, had the aim of translating text from one language to another by computer or other mechanical means. When the MIT Ph.D. program in linguistics was established in 1961, the faculty was, naturally, recruited from among the linguists who were working at MIT and whose experiences had been quite similar to mine. We agreed that in our teaching we would follow the model that we saw all around us at MIT, that of the laboratory group at work on a common problem. The centerpiece of our program would be research in which students and faculty would participate and interact, each according to his or her abilities. To this end we obtained a few offices in Building 20. Unlike the laboratories around us, our offices did not contain special equipment, but they provided space where students could work in a way that did not isolate them from one another; rather, it encouraged them to interact, to review issues that had come up in their classes, and to try out on each other ideas of their own.

This combination of graduate study and research was immensely successful. Students completed their work in relatively short time, and, what was more important, they were enthusiastic about it and communicated their enthusiasm to others. A general effect was that our program was widely copied, and linguistics departments nationwide found space in relatively undesirable real estate and thrived there. A more parochial effect of the success of our teaching methods was that our department tied for first place in the first evaluation of graduate departments conducted by the American Council of Learned Societies in 1965, barely four years after our first graduate students were admitted and MIT linguistics became a going concern. The MIT linguistics program has continued to rank first in the nation in all subsequent polls.

Our teaching methods also had an unanticipated byproduct: They revolutionized the meetings of the various professional societies, first and foremost those of the Linguistic Society of America. Whereas half a century ago it was all but unheard of for a student to speak at such meetings, students are now major participants at all meetings. Members of the society who were active in the 1960s and 1970s will not fail to recall meetings that were enormously enlivened by the interventions of MIT graduate students. And, as I have been told repeatedly, an important reason they were able to overcome the natural diffidence of beginners and talk freely in a big public forum was Building 20, where they had honed their arguments and gained self-confidence in innumerable sessions in their offices.

THE PERMIT THAT the city of Cambridge granted for Building 20 in 1942 was temporary; it anticipated that the building would be dismantled when the war ended. Because MIT didn't urgently need the tract, the university repeatedly persuaded the city to extend the permit, and Building 20 survived into the 1990s. By then, MIT needed a new home for its computer-science department, which almost since its inception has been housed in expensive rental premises. The obvious decision was to replace Building 20 with a new structure appropriate for the many needs of computer science, which at present is arguably the most important area of research and teaching at MIT. In the fall of 1997, just before the old building was closed for demolition, a commemorative meeting was held at MIT. Several hundred mourners, most of whom had begun their careers in the building, came from near and far. Building 20 was demolished in May 1999.

As we bid good-bye to a place that for many of us was home for decades, there have been numerous attempts to put into words the essential qualities of the building. My own suggestion is that in spite of its unprepossessing exterior, Building 20 was a great luxury. It was like money in the bank that could be invested in—or gambled on—projects without guaranteed payoff. The money has now been taken out of the bank and is about to be invested in a spectacular structure designed by Frank Gehry. There are myriad reasons for moving on. The building was beginning to show its age. MIT cannot afford to maintain space that in many ways was substandard. Gehry has promised us a building that will not only look great but also provide for the needs of its inhabitants much better than its predecessor.

Still, there is something to be said for fallow land, for space that not everyone wants to move into, most especially at a place like MIT, where everything moves at top speed and where, according to the local myth, you must be able to take a drink from a fire hose if you want to thrive.

1999

The Spirit
of Maui

REEVE LINDBERGH

"If I take the wings of the morning, and dwell in the
uttermost parts of the sea . . ."

Y FATHER, CHARLES LINDBERGH, IS BURIED IN A
tiny seaside churchyard in Kipahulu, on the island of Maui,
with these words from the 139ᵗʰ Psalm carved in the block of
Vermont granite that marks the deep, wide bed of lava rock
where his coffin was placed almost twenty-five years ago.

It is a traditional Hawaiian grave. My father chose the spot,
and he helped a neighbor and friend, Hawaiian stoneworker
Tevi Kahaleuahi, design the grave. He presided over these
final arrangements even as he lay dying of lymphatic cancer,
at a cottage belonging to other friends, not far from the site.

During that same week, I was told by my brothers who
were there with him, our father enjoyed listening to our
mother's quavering (by her own admission) renditions of
hymns that might be suitable for his upcoming funeral. Once,
when she was singing one of these quietly, thinking he was

napping, he spoke his mind firmly and frankly: "That one's too corny!" She agreed to eliminate it from the plans for the service.

My father's presence of mind was remarkable that August of 1974, although his straightforwardness and practicality were characteristic of the man I had known all my life. Still, for a dying man, he seemed to be in an awfully good mood. The last bill we paid from the time of our father's dying in Maui was one for hamburgers, submitted by Tutu's Hamburger Stand, a snack bar on Hana Bay. Apparently, our father had sent the grave diggers out for a meal at the end of their last day's work, at the end of his life. It struck me as a particularly courteous gesture under the circumstances.

I think he was in an expansive state of mind. My father had, essentially, released himself from modern medicine and state-of-the-art medical technology, having left the New York hospital where he was supposed to be receiving treatment for his advanced cancer, a treatment he had ultimately, politely, refused. Instead, he had arranged to be flown "home" to Hawaii, in the company of his wife and his three sons, none of them knowing whether he would even survive the trip. He did survive it, felt triumphant about the journey, and, despite the weakness of his condition, was completely content to be in Maui and to know that he would always be there, high on a cliff overlooking the Pacific Ocean, with the frigate birds circling above him and the humpback whales breaching below. Then finally, eight days after his last flight, with the grave dug to his specifications and the funeral arrangements made to his satisfaction, my father died. The airman of so many oceans was laid to rest exactly where he had wanted to be, between wings and the sea.

But what was Maui for Charles Lindbergh beyond a place

where my mother and he had built a house on the ocean less than a mile from his eventual grave site? Why this final choice for the son of Swedish immigrants from Minnesota, who bragged to his own children about the cold and snow of midwestern winters as he had known them in the early days of the twentieth century and who loved to confront extremes of weather all over the world? When I was growing up, I would have sworn not only that my father preferred cold weather to warm but also that he distrusted warmth just as he distrusted luxury, and that he too often confused both with simple comfort.

Then why, twenty years later, did he want to move to Maui? Surely, we thought, puzzling over it at the time, Hawaii itself represented everything our father had avoided for a lifetime: tropical weather, crowds, tourists, and luxuries of climate and life that no hardy Scandinavian could tolerate without qualms of conscience and quantities of alarm. It seemed, above all, an enormous change in him, a man of frugal habits and simple tastes. Was he still the father I knew?

The answer, as I have learned over time, is yes, he was— only more so. For I have come to believe that in finding Hawaii, and especially in finding Maui on a visit to a friend in 1968, my father at last retrieved a piece of himself that he had left behind in his own childhood but had never forgotten and never truly relinquished. In fact, in the second and much quieter half of his life, this part of himself, and the values it generated, became more important to him than all of his previous adventures and accomplishments. It left with us, ultimately, what I believe to be his greatest legacy of all.

My father was not of the first but of the second generation in a family of Swedish immigrants who made their way to the United States in the mid-nineteenth century. Through the stories of his own father, who had come to this country when he was a toddler, he shared the pioneers' vision and memory of young America. In a 1969 article called "The Wisdom of Wildness," he wrote, "My father told me about Minnesota's frontier when he was my age. Woods were full of deer, he said, the sky often black with duck; every lake and river held its fish. Chippewa Indians built their tepees near his home. The frontier was a wonderful place for a boy to grow up. He wished I could have been there with him."

As he was growing up, my father absorbed the felt memory of wild land and clean water and open, endless sky. And yet because it was a new and exciting century and his was an adventurous and practical spirit, he eagerly embraced all the new technologies that came his way, from milking machines to motorcycles to automobiles, until finally, in 1922, he took to the air. Up there, "I came to know the world's geography as man had never known it before," he would write.

With knowledge came a new kind of understanding and, over the decades, a growing sense of alarm. He began, in the second half of his life, to consider the disappearance of wilderness and the vanishing of species—including our own—with increasing seriousness. He was by nature and training a scientific thinker, and these drastic eventualities began to seem to him scientifically possible.

In order to try to avert such global disaster, my father changed his life completely as his family watched with astonishment. He turned his attention away from a lifetime of scientific and military pursuits, abandoned the reclusive habits of several decades, and traveled the world, speaking out on behalf of environmental causes. He spoke publicly and cajoled heads of state and public officials in private, even sought out and gave interviews to members of the news media, whom he had avoided with a kind of passion for as long as I had known him. He spoke, as I had never heard him speak before, for the disenfranchised and the powerless, those living beings he considered threatened by the "progress" of civilization in the twentieth century. He spoke for the blue whales in Alaska, for the monkey-eating eagles in the Philippines, and he spoke with growing respect, passion, and understanding for native peoples everywhere.

He said once, in the 1960s, "If I had to choose, I would rather have birds than airplanes," and he said many times that "the human future depends on our ability to combine the knowledge of science with the wisdom of wildness." He had traveled a long distance from his boyhood home in Minnesota, but he had carried its lessons with him all the way.

There was no abandonment of technology, however, no back-to-the-earth retreat into the woods. My father remained a consultant for Pan American Airways for the rest of his life and continued his association with the military as well. He also became involved in and fascinated with the U.S. space program and with space exploration generally, an area of human endeavor he had dreamed about as far back as the early flying days and had pursued with rocket pioneer Robert Goddard in the 1930s.

And yet, despite all his enthusiasm for and identification with the astronauts, this is what my father wrote in 1968 about air and space travel:

> I know I will not return to them, despite limitless possibili-
> ties for invention, exploration, and adventure. Why not?
> Decades spent in contact with science and its vehicles have
> directed my mind and senses to areas beyond their reach. I

now see scientific accomplishments as a path, not an end;
a path leading to and disappearing in mystery.

This, then, was the path my father followed to Maui. It was
not the path of ease or the path of retirement in the usual
sense or even the vacation path we all eagerly follow to the
islands when given the chance. It was the path of mystery. It
began with a sense of ancestral ties to wilderness in his earliest boyhood, carried him brilliantly through many of the
major scientific and technological innovations and explo-
rations of a new century, and gave him wings to cross the
ocean, all alone. Now, drawn by another ocean and another
kind of exploration, his path took him to Maui and the greatest mystery of all.

The last words I ever saw in my father's handwriting during his lifetime were written on a pad of blue airmail paper
that sat on the bedside table in his hospital room in New York
City, before the final flight to Maui. My father was asleep
when I tiptoed into his room, and his sleeping face was paler
and thinner than I had ever seen it. Written on the pad by his
bed, I saw this: "I know there is an infinity outside ourselves.
I wonder now if there is an infinity within, as well."

The move to Maui marked a voyage of the spirit for my father, even before he made his last flight there from the New
York hospital in August 1974. It was a way for him to investi-
gate the "infinity within," to explore and express fully his
growth over seventy years from boy to man, from youth to
age, from scientist to philosopher, from a more practical and
physical to a more abstract and spiritual human being. I did
not know him at the time of the famous flight to Paris in the
1920s or during the tragedy of my brother's kidnapping and
death in the 1930s or during the controversial prewar period

in the early 1940s. I knew him afterward, and felt both awed and privileged to watch for twenty-eight years what was happening to him, and within him, when nobody except his family appeared to be watching him at all. It has occurred to me since that what I was watching in my father those last and hidden years of his life was the final, full development of a human being, a kind of ultimate flowering.

I remember that when my parents lived together in Maui, in the new house they had built in 1969 in Kipahulu, my mother often occupied herself with details of indoor and outdoor housekeeping, as women in my family tend to do when readying a new nest for habitation. My father, though, was most often to be found sitting outdoors on the tiled terrace, just under the sharp eave of the roof, with his back to the house and his face to the ocean. He sat there for hours, watching the whales or the dolphins, looking at the dim outline of the Big Island, Hawaii, faintly visible on the eastern horizon, or just sitting quietly with his notes and papers in his lap, looking out to sea.

There is now an effort under way to preserve this house in Kipahulu. The property was sold after my father's death and then sold again more recently. The latest owners hope to create their own home on the site, and would need to remove or tear down the thirty-year-old original house in order to do so. Individuals and groups interested in the house have suggested several solutions, including a plan to disassemble the original structure and move it piece by piece to a nearby national park that my father helped to establish. This effort has been referred to as the Argonauta project, after the name my parents gave the house, taken from a chapter in my mother's most beloved and best-known book, *Gift from the Sea*. This is the chapter, interestingly enough, in which my mother em-

phasizes the necessity for openness, flexibility, and imperma-
nence, as if in acceptance of the rhythms and patterns of the
later years of life. "We insist on permanency, on duration, on
continuity," one sentence of this chapter reads, "when the
only continuity possible, in life as in love, is in growth, in flu-
idity—in freedom."

Certainly, the final home in Maui was impermanent for my
parents. Though they both loved it, they lived there together
only a few months a year, for fewer than five years. They had,
in fact, little or no history of their own in Maui, although they
were both very much interested in the history of the island itself: the flora and fauna of earth, sea, and sky; the volcanic
origins; and the deep spiritual traditions of Old Hawaii.

My hope is that any preservation efforts for this final home
will not focus on Lindbergh history, because Lindbergh history belongs to other places. My father's boyhood, for instance, has been beautifully remembered at his childhood
home in Minnesota. His famous flight has been extensively,
expertly, and thoroughly documented both by the Missouri
Historical Society in St. Louis and at the Smithsonian Air and
Space Museum in Washington, D.C. Also housed there are the
Lockheed Sirius seaplane *Tingmissartoq* in which my parents
made their survey flights together in the early days and materials relating to those journeys.

If Argonauta is to be preserved, I hope it will be allowed to
be what it was intended to be in the first place: a home not
for Lindbergh history but for Lindbergh values, which developed over a lifetime and found a final haven in that beautiful
spot. I hope it will be a quiet retreat from fame and celebrity.
I hope it will contain and nurture a feeling of being close to
friends and to the natural world. I hope it will be respectful
not just of the Lindberghs who lived there once but also of

their neighbors, who live there still, and of the native traditions that were established in that same place long, long ago. Above all, I hope that Argonauta will remain forever part of the "life of ebb and flow" my mother referred to in a chapter that bears that name: always open to the wings of the morning, always close to the sea.

1999

The Fire This Time

MADISON SMARTT BELL

I N THE FIRST NIGHT OF MY DREAMS I SHUTTLED THE 4 × 4 truck back and forth across the low, dry plain between La Route Nationale 1 and La Route Nationale 3, these being the only two roads that led into the town of Cap Haitien. Both were closed by the demonstrations at La Fossette and Barrière Bouteille, so this semi-secret way between them was of no use, and yet I still kept sewing the two roads together, tighter and tighter with the ever-faster-spinning wheels of the truck, folding and stitching the fabric of the land until it could take no more compression—it must certainly burst. Then in the second night of this dreaming I felt the drums as a pulse in my blood that peeled me out of the battered gray skin of the Montero and fired me like an arrow into the knotted heart of the mapou tree, where the branches twisted out of the trunk like ganglia writhing off the brain stem, the gateway at the base of my skull that would be the spirit's portal of entry. But I woke floundering on the floor of my bedroom in Baltimore, as if some strong force had flung me there, a good long way from Haiti.

THIS TIME, THE summer of the year 2000, I'd come to Cap Haitien with a two-hundred-year-old scene in my head, which I wanted to map onto the actual landscape as accurately as I could. I was at work on a novel about the Haitian Revolution, in which this scene must appear. In 1801, the French colony of Saint Domingue had returned to peace and relative prosperity under the rule of the black general Toussaint L'Ouverture after ten years of sanguinary conflict and disorder, but Napoleon, recently come to power in France, concluded that it would be better to restore slavery in the colony rather than accept the status quo under Toussaint. Soon after, Napoleon sent seventeen thousand of his best troops under the command of his brother-in-law, General Victor Emmanuel Leclerc, to accomplish this mission. Toussaint had anticipated their arrival and had spent all his resources getting ready.

Leclerc appeared with his main force outside the harbor of Le Cap (difficult to navigate without local pilots) and for three days negotiated with Toussaint's subordinate, General Henri Christophe, who refused to allow him unopposed entry to the city. Le Cap (known to the ancien régime as Cap Français) had been burned to the ground, during an earlier stage of the Haitian Revolution, in 1793. Since then the town had been rebuilt to an even more opulent standard by revolutionary slaves, and deserved its sobriquet "the Pearl of the Antilles" even more than before. When Leclerc attempted to force a landing, Christophe set fire to the town again, beginning with his own palatial residence; as he'd promised, he left the French general nothing but a field of cinders. So began the final war of the Haitian Revolution, which ended with the expulsion of the French and with Haitian independence.

Since colonial times, a narrow ravine (now functioning as an open sewer) has divided the main area of Le Cap from the mountains behind it and from the several blocks tucked in between the cliffs and the waterfront collectively known as

Le Carénage. I found a bridge that led to the winding drive ascending Morne Calvaire, now surmounted by a seminary and its chapel, Sainte Thérèse de la Croix. Below the steep semicircular stairs that rose to the church door, Christ crucified overlooked the town from the brow of the hill, flanked by broken plaster statues of the executed thieves. Below, whitecaps rushed over the harbor, and the wind was stiff in my face as I stood on the hill. I could see past the rose-colored tiles of the old colonial rooftops fanning away among the more recently, sloppily erected structures, past the place d'Armes and the eighteenth-century cathedral, destroyed during the Leclerc invasion and restored by Henri Christophe in 1811, all the way to Barrière Bouteille and beyond. Miles further, atop one of the most difficult peaks of the mountain range that closed the horizon, the silhouette of La Citadelle was just discernible. The colossal fortress was also begun around 1811 by Christophe, once he had become king of the northern part of Haiti, as a last redoubt against any possible return of the French. Another year, I'd made the daylong climb up Morne La Ferrière to the fortress and along the way been presented with a corroded button from the coat of one of Christophe's soldiers: Embossed with a phoenix, it bore the legend JE RENAIS DE MES CENDRES ("I am reborn from my ashes").

Burning is still in style in Cap Haitien, though not on the revolutionary scale. Le Cap remains the most significant surviving town from the colonial Caribbean, delicately balanced on the cusp between destruction and preservation. There exists a thoroughly detailed and well articulated code for historic preservation of colonial buildings, created by the Institut de Sauvegarde du Patrimoine National (ISPAN)—the organization whose greatest achievement to date has been the magnificent restoration completed in 1990 of La Citadelle itself. But most of the people who are able to purchase buildings in *l'ancienne ville* are disinclined to abide by those regulations, which may be evaded by burning down the house and then building something more contemporary on the scorched lot. Word on the street was that much of this arson was the work of drug dealers, Le Cap, with its large harbor, being an important transshipment point between producers in Latin America and consumers in the United States.

In a period when most of the legitimate economy had been brought to a standstill by political deadlock, the drug traffickers were more appreciated than loathed by the populace, since their activities, however unenlightened with regard to historic preservation, provided a significant proportion of what little employment was available. One of them famously distributed the equivalent of twenty dollars to all the misfortunate people of his neighborhood on the same day every week, an effective investment in his own security, since a whisper against him in that part of town would certainly set off a riot.

Cap Haitien is nowhere near as catastrophically overpopulated as the capital, Port-au-Prince, but *l'ancienne ville,* its geographic area more or less fixed by the boundaries of mountains, sea, and the marshy ground outside the gates, has come under increasing pressure from the population of slums and shantytowns mushrooming in those same unhealthy swamplands in the area of La Fossette (the former colonial cemetery). ISPAN had cooperated in a plan to relocate those people on higher, drier, and healthier terrain somewhat farther from town, but due to governmental deadlock, this idea had not been executed, so the pressure on the old town continued to mount.

In the summer of 1999, ISPAN opened a new headquarters
in the midst of its own project to renovate a colonial hospital
on just the other side of the ravine below Morne Calvaire.
That had been a relatively optimistic season, when it seemed
that such projects might advance more quickly. The structure
is a long, rectangular enclosure running down the slope, with
single-story, barrackslike accommodations built inward from
the walls. Under both the regime of Jean-Claude Duvalier and
the de facto military junta that launched the 1991 coup
against Aristide, the building was used as a prison. During
dechoukage (the period following the fall of Duvalier, when
many Duvalierist institutions were uprooted by the people),
it had been liberated by a mob that stayed on as squatters for
a time. One of their slogans was still spray painted on the
wall: *Youn sel nou fèb/ Ansanm nou fò/ Ansanm Ansanm
n'ap rive.* ("Alone we're weak/ Together we're strong/ All together we'll get there.")

I pushed through the iron gate an hour before sundown.
The enclosure was quiet, calm, almost deserted, with a few
men sitting on curbstones under the shade of tall mango trees
and palms that the surrounding walls had for many years protected from scavengers. The renovation seemed to have pro-
gressed little since the previous year—sucked into the
doldrums of governmental stasis. I waited for my sweat to
dry, then walked up the slope toward the main offices. There
were stacks of cement blocks, and a few defunct vehicles
partly overgrown with weeds. I met one of the ISPAN orga-
nizers, on his way home for the day, and we chatted for a few
minutes, leaning on the tailgate of one of the operational
jeeps. Since last year, the mood had turned back toward frustration. ISPAN had always had difficulties with the town government, which was disinclined to enforce the preservation

code; the code had legal status, but after all, there was little law enforcement of any kind anywhere in Haiti. A succession of mayors had brought no improvement, and this year a whole section of the center of the town had been almost entirely demolished. My visit was sandwiched between two legislative elections, and I voiced the possibility that the problems in Le Cap might finally begin to be more addressable once a president was elected in the fall. My interlocutor muttered that the fall election might represent some chance, and then added that it would be the last chance, too.

THIS MOOD OF frustration was general then; it entered with the air you breathed. One of my Haitian friends had managed to buy, last summer, a tiny plot of land in the countryside of Morne Rouge. It was a stone's throw from the sacred mapou tree of Bwa Cayman, which commemorated the first full-scale slave insurrection at the beginning of the revolution, in 1791. He'd set about planting trees himself, including a mapou seedling, but everything had died in the drought. There was one substantial *manguier* on the property; this year it bore no fruit, because the neighbors had cut back the limbs for charcoal. Such acts were born out of desperation and only made the circle tighter and tighter, more and more vicious; if the trend could not somehow be reversed, the whole country would strangle itself.

It was understood that trees made water; a Kreyòl proverb advises that if you want water, you must not cut the trees by your spring. Moreover, trees were understood to be *reposoirs,* or resting places, for the spirits.

L'arbre respire comme l'homme, my friend told me—"the tree breathes the same as man"—and from this principle flows the spiritual and medicinal element of Vodouisant (voodoo) practice. The neighbors said that the big mango tree was inhabited by a snake and claimed that they wanted to cut it down for that reason, but surely they must have recognized the serpent as the embodiment of the *lwa* Damballah, the Vodou deity often incarnate in snakes. I think they wanted to cut the tree to raise a little cash from the charcoal it would make.

In the hammered gray Montero, I played over and over a beautiful sad song by the group Wawa—all drums and voices: *Figuier, mapou yo/ yo tout fin peri o/ pa gegne youn kote anko/ pou lwa yo rete.* ("The fig trees and maples/ They've all just now died/ There is no place anymore/ For the spirits to stay.")

It was true, and the problem of Le Cap's colonial architecture seemed small beside it. In the year 2000, the whole Haitian environment was still just barely salvageable, but only if something was done effectively, and soon. In the midst of the political paralysis, the last chance was slipping away, and if you dwelled upon this point, your entrails would be gnawed from the inside out with sadness.

I'M SO HAPPY!, the young man told me, speaking English, which suggested he might have come from the States for the ceremonies—the *fête,* as it was casually called: the party. His face was black and gleaming with sweat and energy, happiness, really, as he claimed: I'm so happy! He kept bouncing toward me and away like a Superball, while I nodded and grinned, no more than mildly uncomfortable in my white skin this year. Dozens like him dominated the area under the drums in the first few nights of the ceremonies, young men half transported by the drums and half drunk on the raw white rum called *clairin. Vakabons,* as they might be called elsewhere, bad guys, but their aggression had no real edge on it here; it was just a game. They really were happy, though some of them were there all night because they had nowhere else to go. It seemed everyone else was there, too, or at least most classes of Cap Haitien were represented: There were young girls dressed for dancing, alone or in pairs (the *vak-abons* did not molest or pester them either; a strong decorum obtained amid the apparent abandon), and cripples on crutches, hobbling old men, old women who could still dance light as butterflies, many people emaciated by a life-time of near starvation, others prosperous enough to be fat. There was food and drink aplenty for those who could buy; the market women ringed the sanctuary with their coolers shrouded in burlap, trays of wrapped candies and Comme Il Faut cigarettes, iron cauldrons of meat and rice and beans. In the center, circled by a line of shuffling chanting dancers, was a long table laid with a *manje lwa*—a tower of liquor bottles and fancy cakes and other comestibles mounting up to a sac-rifice to feed the spirits whom the drums and the singing in-vited.

This temple itself, the *hounfor,* was a power node, a place for the spirits to focus and erupt. It lay tucked on a path that led from behind the church and continued, on the other side of the *hounfor,* past a cliffside site said to be inhabited by the spirits of the Taino Indians, whom the Spanish occupants of Hispaniola had exterminated. The Taino strain braided into Vodou reinforces the idea of spirits inhabiting particular places: The site may be a tree or a rock or a drum or a spring, which the spirit takes for its *reposwa.* On the streets below were the old points of colonial power—the barracks and the governor's residence—and beyond them was the sea itself, rushing under the ripening moon, understood by Vodouisants to be a mirror surface that divides the world of the living from the world of the dead. Rochambeau, the last French general in Saint Domingue, had drowned so many in the harbor of Le Cap that the townspeople gave up eating fish for fear that they might be eating their relatives. There in *Ginen anba dlo,* "Africa beneath the waters," was the great spiritual reservoir collectively known as Les Morts et Les Mystères, which absorbed the spirit of anyone who ever died in Haiti, including all the heroes of the revolution: Jean-Jacques Dessalines and Christophe and Toussaint L'Ouverture and the others, whose names were not recorded or remembered.

I was here to invite those spirits to arise in me, if they were willing, and use my body as an instrument of passage so they might move and act and speak again in the world of the living. If everyone at the ceremonies this year was exceptionally kind to me, I think it was because my intention was clear. I passed below the drums, and one of the drummers brought me into the rhythm of his beat, stroking my shoulders several times with his mallet, and one of the singers raised me on the other side and shared his microphone with me, feeding the Kreyòl words of the song into my ear so that I might give my voice to the chorus chanting the young woman in the white minidress into the vortex of possession. I passed behind the drums, pausing a moment to clash a loose pair of irons to the beat. As I reached the left side of the drummers, it seemed that a spirit shot through me to lodge in the woman just ahead; she had not been dancing or demonstrating in any way but was taken with a moan and a soft collapse. She dropped back against me, and I steadied her head with my right hand and had, for a moment, the privilege of supporting her, her arms outstretched in the form of the cross.

.   .   .

I TOOK MY friend Andy with me to Fort Picolet: insurance in case one of my two trick knees should give way on the narrow path that wrapped along the cliff, beyond Le Carénage to the point commanding the approach into the harbor. The fort was a ruin, but many of its walls and stairways were still standing. Ancient cannons lay dismounted behind the battlements, and Andy showed me a circular well-like shaft that he said had been used as a dungeon.

Below the fort, just above the waterline, a freshwater spring ran out of the razor-edged lava formations of the *côte de fer*. I inched my way down, past a small group of young people seated on the rocks. At first they put me in mind of the students one saw everywhere studying on the street, often profiting from the lights of private generators when the state electricity was blacked out. But as I crawled down past them, I saw that what one of them was writing was a dense, letterless scrawl that would finally obliterate the page (this would become, perhaps, a secret society passport), and the song they were singing was for Damballah. I stooped to touch my fingers to the spring and wet the space at the base of my skull with the fresh water, then soaked my red head cloth and retied it with the wet knot just there at the basal ganglia. *"Fok w bwe youn coup tou,"* one of the people on the rock remarked as I climbed back past them—"you ought to drink a shot also"—but it seemed I wasn't ready to take that last step, though I was grateful for the suggestion.

I had been soaked to the waist by a rogue wave erupting like a geyser through a hole in the rock, so we paused on one of the upper stairways of the fort, where I could spread my shoes and socks to dry in the brilliant sun. While we rested, Andy told me that sometimes the ocean sends a bladelike

wave to punish someone who served the spirits with insuffi-
cient faith or diligence. He told me that the spring was the *reposwa* of Ezili Fréda, the kinder, gentler aspect of a goddess
something like a Haitian Aphrodite, and that higher on the
pathway where we'd halted was the *reposwa* of Ezili Je Rouj:
the enraged and outraged Red-Eyed Ezili, driven wild by her
losses and her terrible, unbearable disappointments; she
ripped at her hair and her clothing and tore at the ground itself with her nails. At that I said we would go no farther; I did
not wish to encounter Ezili Je Rouj. Ah, said Andy, *"li pa
bon?"* And I replied quickly, "No, I didn't say she wasn't
good; I only say that I don't mean to call her."

It was calm and bright where we were sitting, for the moment as peaceful as anyone might imagine. On the water
below, a tour boat from the Royal Caribbean cruise resort at
Labadie Beach had come about to face the fort, and one of the
wealthy lords of the town skimmed over the surface of the
ocean in his powerboat. A rarely seen great frigate bird
wheeled on its long wings above the battlements where two
hundred years before the first shot was fired on one of
Leclerc's ships, the signal for Christophe to set the town on fire.

ON SATURDAY NIGHT the drums were silent in the *hounfor,*
and the moon was dark. Saturday morning, supposed to be
my last day in Haiti, I drove out through La Fossette onto the
flat expanse of the plain, looking for Habitation Héricourt, a
plantation that Toussaint had acquired during the revolution
and briefly used as a headquarters in the first days of Leclerc's
invasion. No one could tell me just where it had been, but I
was getting the general sense of the landscape, the lush low-
land bristling with sugarcane, now and then interrupted by a
grove of bananas or mango trees, here and there a breadfruit

tree or a *corrosol,* and all the hedgerows purply, laced with
bougainvillea. It was almost surreally calm and still, and
when I picked up my friend at Bréda, he told me that people
had begun throwing stones and bottles in the area of Cité Le-
scot, between us and Le Cap. Our program called for us to go
back that way, but we were repelled by a wall of black
smoke; they'd already set the tires on fire and closed the
road, a mile out from Barrière Bouteille. I pulled a bootleg
turn, and we headed, with all deliberate speed, back the way
we'd come, toward the lesser-known road that connected the
two highways across the plain. There was a limit to how fast
this crossing could be made, due to potholes, washboards,
sinkholes, scattered boulders, and other such obstacles, but I
held our speed near the maximum; and it was shake, rattle,
and roll till we regained the pavement of Route 3 and turned
quickly toward the town again. We hadn't passed a word between us, said nothing to admit there might be a problem,
and in fact all seemed calm enough until we reached Kalfou
La Fossette. There, the central circle had been set ablaze, but
the barricades had not yet been dragged across the intersection, nor had the mob yet filled the street.

"Fais ça rapidement!" my friend hissed at me, and I
whipped the truck around that flaming geyser and made it
through, into the town and safe at last, or so I thought, but
the last snare was timed exactly for that moment of relief, the
lapse of attention when I let my hand fall on my friend's
knee, congratulating him on our safe passage: Just beneath
my wheels appeared a whole blockful of broken beer bottles
standing on end, clawing like the angry nails of Ezili Je Rouj
herself. By the grace of God I saw the trap in time to miss it
by a hair, and we skimmed past into the free, safe zone of the
waterfront and the boulevard de la Mer.

Of course I'd been expecting trouble; I just wasn't expecting it that day. The run-up to the next week's election was bound to bring on demonstrations of some kind, but since an important object of the flaming barricades was to freeze traffic on a workday, they usually didn't happen on the weekend. I'd bet too heavily on that principle. This time around, Ezili Je Rouj was bound to manifest herself whether anyone explicitly called her or not; her spirit was the spirit in the air.

That night I went up to the Hôtel Mont Joli, on another low hilltop nearby Morne Calvaire, to pick up gossip and calculate my chances of making it out to the airport the next day. For the time being, the town was sealed and the whole northern region cut off from the capital; demonstrators had felled trees across the road at Dondon and welded the bridge shut at Limbé. It looked like I was settling in for a several-day siege. Word on the street was that the demonstrators came from the opposition to Fanmi Lavalas, Aristide's party, and that they were in the pay of the Americans. Another story had it that the demonstrators were Lavalas themselves, demanding that the results of the May elections (where they'd won almost universal victory) be made immediately official. An Organization of American States election observer I spoke to believed that the demonstration was a reaction to the challenge his mission had issued to the method by which the election results were calculated . . . and no one knew anything for certain. From where I sat at the bar of the Mont Joli, I could see the flames leaping into the dark sky beyond La Fossette and Barrière Bouteille. A boon from the research point of view, for it gave some idea of what it must have looked like when the first fires were started in Le Cap in 1793, and again in 1802. Some Haitians called the movement that brought Aristide and his party to power the Second Revolution, for something in the First Revolution had been left incomplete and unfulfilled. Thus the rage, frustrated disappointment, the spirit of Ezili Je Rouj abroad in the streets one more time. From where I sat, I thought they might be right: Those fires were two hundred years old tonight, and they were burning still.

2001

On the Dock of
the Bay

SOMETIMES AT NIGHT I WALK OUT OF MY COTTAGE deep beneath the oaks on Mobile Bay and head down to the water's edge. Having been a city dweller for many years, I've never been one to study the constellations, but residing now on the Alabama coast, with the Southern sky spread above me, I've been peeking into a book by H. A. Rey—not his whimsical *Curious George,* but his gently instructive *The Stars.* His connect-the-dot drawings, Castor and Pollux hand in hand, enliven the heavens I can see from this spot. When I face south, toward the mouth of the bay, Scorpius unfurls off the end of our pier; Antares flickers red at its heart. The North Star holds firm behind me, a reminder of New York, my previous home.

If I stroll up the boardwalk to the tip of Point Clear, I come to the Grand Hotel, a 150-year-old resort villa of green wooden cottages tucked in along paths, hotel rooms in two long, red-roofed wings of the main lodge, and immense picture windows opening on the water. From the hotel's band shell, echoing at least for me of last Saturday night's swing band, I look up the bay to where the Big Dipper seems to pour out on the port of Mobile. At this distance, the lights of the Alabama State Docks' coal chutes, loading ramps, whirly-bird cranes, and barges seem festive—a vision that belies the hard, round-the-clock labor that goes on there.

There are other constellations I'm learning to read—the string of lights on Fairhope Pier on my side of the bay, the pinpoints of Dog River Bridge on the other. Turning south again, I see the flicker of a radio tower at Dauphin Island, our coastal barrier island. In the Gulf of Mexico beyond are natural-gas rigs bright as tiny casinos, their payoffs and risks just as high. Like Antares, a red light flickers, answered by a flash of green. Two by two, the lights mark the channel from the port of Mobile to the wooden platform lighthouse of Mid-dle Bay Light to the clanging sea buoy far out in the Gulf, where the big ships anchor.

I grew up near this bay in the city of Mobile in the 1950s and 1960s. Every summer my family would pack up the car, pass through the Bankhead Tunnel at the foot of Government Street downtown, cross the causeway to our Eastern Shore: Daphne, Montrose, Fairhope, Point Clear, Mullet Point. Al-though it has been long superseded by a stretch of elevated I-10, the causeway is a road I still prefer. Tin-shed fishing camps with BAIT signs scrawled in front, seafood shacks on stilts, men standing patiently by the sea walls holding cane poles over the water—its scenery has not changed much in the four decades I've been traversing it.

The bay houses we rented for a few weeks each summer varied from simple bungalows far down the shore to grand affairs with sleeping porches, plank floors, and ten-foot ceil-ings at Point Clear. Each house had its own pier. I remember pulling up crab traps with my sister, trawling for shrimp with my father, doing cannonballs off the end of the pier with my friends. Sometimes we kids slept out at the pier's end, listening to the swirl and splash of fish feeding all night long as we waited for a jubilee—a rare phenomenon of this estuary, where crabs, shrimp, or flounder swim groggily near the shore for a few hours. One summer I learned how to cast a mullet net from a caretaker who lived across the road and used to appear at sunrise at waterside, hurling circles of net onto the lurking and leaping fish.

I took in the rhythms of the bay: its mirror calm at sunrise; its humid mid-morning, when shrimp boats seemed motionless on the horizon; its lunchtime, when families gathered to eat crab claws and seafood gumbo on the big, screened porches of raised cottages; its late afternoons, when cumulus clouds, on four o'clock cue, closed out the sun and sent gulls hurtling before them. Lightning that cracked at the windows, then sunsets that bathed the porches—I remember those, too.

Then I went to college and headed north and stayed away for a long time, except for visits home. The bay, for me, became a vast well of memory from which I'd draw recollections for my friends in New York. But until 1996, when I took a writing job in Mobile and returned with my wife and daughter to rent year-round on the bay, I did not realize how little I knew about the other lives unfolding here. The bay was no longer just a setting for hammock swings against painterly sunsets; it became a place of daily commerce and backbending toil and traumatic history. Like H. A. Rey's tales of stellar twins and scorpions animating the skies, the stories I've been told by bar pilots, fisherman, dockworkers, and those with blood ties to the water make the bay come alive too.

THE MOBILE BAR Pilots Association was founded in 1865, a date I'm reminded of whenever I wear their cap, which also displays an anchor, a ship's wheel, and the flag of Alabama.

For several days, researching a story, I trailed after Captain G. Wildon Mareno, a third-generation bar pilot whom I met up with at the pilots' dispatch center at the Alabama State Docks. Mareno also grew up in Mobile but navigated tankers for Texaco for twenty years, sailing the world. When a slot opened up with the Mobile bar pilots, he returned home and now heads up the association.

On call every other week, the bar pilots are contacted by the dispatcher by phone. In the time of Mareno's father and grandfather, though, they took two-week shifts living aboard a schooner in the Gulf, near the entrance to Mobile Bay. Then, as now, they'd meet oceangoing vessels coming to port in Mobile, taking over the helm to navigate them past treacherous sandbars into the bay's channel.

Late one windy night I drove with Mareno from the State Docks out to Dauphin Island. At a bunkhouse the pilots maintain there, I napped until two o'clock in the morning, when he shook me awake and handed me a life vest. We boarded a sixty-five-foot launch that plied six-foot swells, carrying us out to a huge freighter near the bell-clanging sea buoy. The ship was registered in Cyprus; its captain was a Filipino. Only a Mobile bar pilot could bring the deep-hulled vessel into port. A rope ladder slid down the side of the freighter. Mareno, fifty-four, scaled it nimbly, casting an eye down to make sure that the younger reporter who'd insisted on shadowing him had not lost heart or stomach. As I climbed the thirty feet up the iron hull, with the ship already under way, I looked down just once to see the pilot's launch falling away beneath us, bobbing like a cork.

On board, lit by the glow of the instrument panels, Mareno took charge, beginning the three-and-a-half-hour trip to the port of Mobile and a final docking assisted by harbor tugs. I'd gone deep-sea fishing in these waters many times, but I'd never looked out at night from the wheelhouse of a ship. Sand Island lighthouse, long a bright beam, was dark. Sand Island itself, once an offshore stretch of wilderness popular with campers, was a fragment of tiny islands, cut to pieces by years of hurricanes. On one side of Mobile Bay's entrance stood the Civil War fortress of Fort Gaines, with its high brick walls, turrets, and cannons. On the other was the promontory of Fort Morgan, rising from the dunes. Somewhere beneath us was the USS *Tecumseh,* sent to the bottom in the Civil War battle of Mobile Bay, still awaiting salvage.

All went well until the fog rolled in and the red and green channel markers disappeared. Mareno kept track of other vessels by radar, blasting the foghorn. We heard another foghorn answering us dead ahead. The captain knew that the approaching ship was being navigated by a fellow bar pilot, and they radioed back and forth. The fog had surprised them, he explained to me, which can happen, since it does not show up on the radar. They never set out if socked in by fog. He calculated numbers that made me understand one reason why. Our ship was 72 feet wide at the beam and weighed 10,000 tons. The approaching craft was 62 feet wide and weighed 6,500 tons. The channel was 400 feet wide. If either freighter, to avoid the other, steered too close to the channel's edge, the water pressure would build against the hull with a shearing effect, pushing its bow out across the middle of the channel, risking a collision. There was no room for error.

The other ship loomed out of nowhere like the edge of a cliff; silently, it slid by us, then disappeared into the fog.

THE ALABAMA-TOMBIGBEE river system empties into the port of Mobile. At the Alabama State Docks, a complex of ware-

houses, loading berths, and train yards, I spent time with
some longshoremen, following them from the union hall,
where a work gang was chosen by a weathered foreman
nicknamed Hook (for his reputed ability to grab cargo off
railcars with his bare hands), to the loading dock alongside a
seven-hundred-foot-long transport ship. Their objective: to
load nineteen thousand tons of wood pulp into the hold of
the vessel, bound for Japan. Through a long weekend they
labored, changing shifts with other work gangs, around the
clock. I peered into the hold of the ship, watching bales of
pulp, wired into thirty-ton loads, being lowered to the workers by a gantry crane. The men looked small and vulnerable,
trusting in the safety of the machine. The ship got lower in
the water; the bales of wood pulp got higher. Suddenly a wire
came loose as a load was high in the air. There were shouts
as two of the bales dangled precariously. But the load was
lowered back to the dock, refastened securely, and lifted up
and over the hold of the ship again.

On their lunch breaks, as gulls stole bread crumbs from the
ground, the longshoremen showed me their wounds. One
wiry old-timer had an S-scar on his palm where his hand had
been crushed between a crate and a connecting hook. Another fellow told of a man whose foot was smashed when an
iron pipe rolled against him; the storyteller himself walked
with a limp. A husky, broad-shouldered man in his fifties recalled the summer of 1960, when he came south from a rural
county in Alabama and began working at the docks. In tan-
dem with another worker, he'd haul 140-pound sacks of fer-
tilizer and 100-pound sacks of corn and rice. They'd trudge to
the side of the ship and hurl the sacks upward to another
worker, who'd stack them twelve high. The forklift, he explained philosophically, now does what a man's back used to

do. He did not rue those hard days of dock labor, telling me it had been better than picking cotton up in the country, and with better pay.

"My uncles came back from Mobile and told us about it," he recalled. "To us it was a little piece of heaven."

IN 1859, SHORTLY before the Civil War, a ship bringing slaves to America from the kingdom of Dahomey in West Africa made its way across Mobile Bay. The importation of slaves was by then a violation of federal law; the captain of the ship, arriving in the port of Mobile, took the slaves off and scuttled the vessel by setting fire to it, hiding evidence of the voyage. I'd heard this story of the *Clotilda* many times over the years, but it was not until I began to live on Mobile Bay that I grew interested in the families whose lives had been most affected by the journey, the descendants of the *Clotilda*'s slaves. Those slaves, either abandoned to fend for themselves, legend says, or freed after the Civil War, had formed a community called Africatown along the Mobile River near the port. The author Zora Neale Hurston visited it early this century, gathering stories of the most well known *Clotilda* passenger, Cudjo "Kazoola" Lewis. The church these survivors founded exists still.

I sought out descendants of Cudjo, among them a seventy-five-year-old great-granddaughter, Martha West Davis, who spent time with him as a little girl and can still recall his animal-skin shoes and taste his fish-and-tomato stews. Another descendant, Israel Lewis III, teaches art to schoolchildren—and life lessons to offenders in juvenile boot camps—inspired by the life of Cudjo. He told me of an ancestral handshake passed on from African forebears that his own father had given him from his deathbed. Lewis felt a "jolt" in that final grasp, a force of energy, he believed, linking him directly to Cudjo. He clasped my forearm in his hand to demonstrate. I felt only a strong grip, but it was not my ancestry to receive.

SAY THE NAMES Camille, Frederic, Opal, and Erin on Mobile Bay and you'll hear stories about hurricanes. I'll be the old-timer one day, jawboning about one called Danny. My wife and I, both natives, know to be wary of big storms, but we felt secure tucked far enough away from the Gulf of Mexico in July 1997. We figured we'd lose our electrical power, so we gathered candles, canned food, transistor radios, and bottles of water. We gassed up the car just in case. The Creole cottage we live in sits well behind a big two-story house fronting the bay. It's usually occupied by vacationers, but not during the storm. Our next-door neighbors, permanent residents, had built a new brick house that could withstand even the Big Bad Wolf. They offered us shelter in the event that our cottage started to shake.

Before the weather reporters could tell us that Danny was churning closer—the power did go out and the TV screen went blank—the frogs told us. All through the woods along Mobile Bay they began to croak a nervous symphony. Soon they were bellowing. The winds bent saplings double, yanked the limbs off oaks, turned the eaves of the house into a musical instrument—a French horn, a bassoon. The water lashed the sides of my daughter's bedroom, and she huddled with us in ours.

Past hurricanes have left their mark on this bay. Every morning I look out at a public pier where ferries docked in the early part of this century. Wrecked by a long-ago storm, only its pilings remain, a haunt for fishermen. The opposite shore knows a sadder story, in the old resort community of

Coden. Scores drowned there in the 1906 hurricane—a tragedy like the San Francisco earthquake of the same year, one that still reverberates through families.

For an entire day Danny took up residence on Mobile Bay. When the eye passed over us, I hurried out in the brief calm. A low tide and swirling wind had not created a storm surge but had instead driven the water far out. Beneath the pier the bottom was pocked, lunar. Then the winds picked up again, and rains poured down like the Big Dipper letting loose. The tide began to shift, and I raced inside. By the time Danny moved on to Pensacola, we had opened the door and sloshed through the yard, stepping over downed tree limbs. Pelicans reappeared and took up sentry positions on the tops of boat pilings. We went to the shore, strewn with driftwood and sea grass, and looked out at the choppy water bright again with the insistent sun. I'd grown up on Mobile Bay but felt that I'd only now arrived.

1998

Something There Is
That Loves a Wall

NOEL PERRIN

THE PIECE OF LAND IN CENTRAL VERMONT I SOMEWHAT misleadingly call my farm contains only ninety acres. But on those few acres I have about 160,000 ornamental stones.

With twenty-three exceptions, none of these stones has been shaped by human hands. They still look just as they did when the glacier left them here. Even the twenty-three are plain and simple. My farm has no sculpture garden, or even a marble birdbath. Four of the shaped stones are granite doorsteps, two of them leading to the front door of my old brick farmhouse and two that lead to the kitchen door. But plain as they are—mere rectangles of smooth stone—they do give a kind of visual crispness to the front of the house. And in 180 years they haven't sagged a bit, or even visibly worn. My heart gives a little skip whenever I see them (which, of course, is several times a day).

The other nineteen exceptions are all cut-granite fence posts, much more roughly finished than the steps, though just as old. Five of them continue to do their duty in holding up a section of pasture fence; the rest are broken pieces that I have incorporated in retaining walls. They make terrific accent marks.

I might as well confess that most of them I stole—though you could also say I redeemed them. Twenty years ago they were lying on the ground, along the roadside boundary of a disused cemetery two villages away. Once, that cemetery had been entirely fenced with granite posts and wooden rails. Long ago an occasional post began to snap off at ground level, usually when a snowplow or careless bulldozer hit it. That ended its service as a post. Now it just lay there, choked in weeds. I feared that these broken tops might eventually sink out of sight—or, worse, get taken to a sanitary landfill. So I rescued them. One person can, though just barely, lift a piece of stone like that into the back of a pickup truck, or at least tip one end up onto the tailgate and then wiggle it in. In three night visits, I rescued all fourteen that had snapped off.

But what about the other 159,977 ornamental stones? Well, one is a glacial monolith the size of two UPS trucks. It lies deep in what are now woods. Its special feature is a cleft about two feet wide that runs clear through it and in which a century-old white birch grows. Long ago, but still after the woods took over the fields that were once there, children converted that great stone into a fort. They walled up both entrances, and also a side cleft, to a height of about three feet. My children used that fort, and I have a seventy-year-old neighbor who tells me *he* used it when he was a small boy. The birch was already big then.

All the rest are built into stone walls. Together they form just over two miles of wall, and they are the chief glory of my farm. What's best about them is that they follow so perfectly the lay of the land. One curls up over the flank of a hill—and becomes the grace of the hill made visible. Another forms a stone contour line running about a hundred feet below the top of the farm's highest hill. All respond to the land as a really talented dancer does to a partner. Only, the walls do it forever.

Well, not quite forever. But for centuries. There are tumbledown sections, I admit, a few of which I have repaired and most of which I haven't. But a full mile, I'd say, has retained almost every stone, and those walls still show the aesthetics of their builders undiminished. I'm thinking of places where the wall rises to meet the bulk of an incorporated monolith and sinks down once past it, or where big stones have been placed so nicely in relation to each other that one almost has a duty to get a pad and make a sketch. Provided one can sketch.

Most of the walls are very old, but there are also three new ones. I built them. Two are short retaining walls—my prentice work. One's about thirty yards long, the other hardly twenty. But the third one! It runs the full length of my best cow pasture adorning the whole east side, replacing the rusted barbed wire that held cows in a couple of owners back.

This is no prentice job. I paced the length of that wall just now, and it comes to 184 paces, or about 175 yards. I got the stones for it chiefly by prying them up in two little rocky pastures farther back—and I was choosy in what I took. Rejects went to plug a gully that must have started around 1890. Someone plowed a little too near the edge of a slope.

I didn't have to reject many, though. Once you get away from the river bottoms, my part of central Vermont is not particularly rich land, but it *is* well supplied with good stone. The rock is nine-tenths granite—very little ugly shale or incongruous quartz—and it's flat granite at that. Nearer flat than round, anyway. No stone cannonballs, such as Robert Frost complains of in the poem "Mending Wall." Two out of three stones go nicely in a wall, and I could often have put the third one in, too, if I weren't indulging a late-blooming perfectionist streak.

It took five years to build that wall, working at odd moments. Mostly they were cool dawns of what were going to be hot summer days. Sometimes I had help. For three years the village doctor worked with me. We did a couple of hours every Wednesday morning, one week on a wall at his place, the next week on mine. We both saved big stones up for when the other would be there.

And once I had still more extensive help, which is how there comes to be a named stone in that wall. A friend in the next village—a summer person—had agreed to put up three touring Oxford students. Then, as often happens to summer people, he got summoned away on short notice. Had to give some kind of talk in Pennsylvania. He asked me if I would put up the three Oxonians for their last two nights, and I said sure.

I hadn't expected the bonus this produced. The three of them announced that before they left they were going to put in a morning of farmwork for me. I chose wall work. During that morning we placed half a dozen substantial stones in the long wall: 300-pounders, 500-pounders. The biggest of all is called the Oxford Stone, and a fine shapely piece of granite it is.

It's in a different wall altogether, one I merely rebuilt, that the Mary Faeth Perch appears, named after a young cousin who spent a good part of one college weekend working on that wall with me. A *perch*, incidentally, is the same as a rod, which is the same as 16½ feet. *Rod* is used more for road widths and *perch* more for wall lengths, though neither is used much at present. But I like to preserve them.

There's also the Ursula Gibson Half-Perch, in yet another wall. Ursi worked on that with me one spring afternoon her senior year in college. She's now both a mother and an associate professor of engineering at Dartmouth. Mary Faeth is now a lecturer in outdoor education in Australia. None of this history appears on any sign or plaque. The meaning of these stones lives entirely in the memory, as landmarks did for Indians.

But back to the long wall, the one I built from scratch. It is, I think, a thing of beauty. But it is also a highly practical wall. It really does hold cows in, unaided by barbed wire, cyclone fence, electric fence, underground Kow-Stop, and so on. Nor is it alone in doing this. Directly opposite it, on the west side of that pasture, there's a fine old retaining wall, way too high for even Angus cattle to jump. I've patched it a little—but probably less than ten hours' worth in the thirty years I've lived here.

Many of the other stone pasture fences are much lower—there's one stretch that's not even three feet. I did once see two lonesome Angus steers jump *that* so as to join a cluster of pretty heifers on the other side. In such places I do indeed use barbed wire—but far less than I'd use if there were no stone wall, and stretched on lighter posts. The stones are still working.

To me that's the most important thing about my walls. They contain 160,000 ornamental stones, and all of them work, or could work. That's how it should be. Beauty, in my opinion, almost always should work, and work should try always to be beautiful.

The division between practical and beautiful, so taken for granted in current life, isn't even an old one. With minor exceptions, it dates only to the seventeenth century. Prior to that, nearly everything was both. Sicilian farmers spent a lot of time decorating their farm carts—which didn't increase the capacity by a single ounce. Medieval armor was part body protection, part mobile art. Castles were to be impregnable and also to look glorious and romantic, especially in their curtain walls, bastions, crenellations, and battlements. That's one reason kids love them so much.

Even paintings, most of them, were part aesthetic, part for use. Van Eyck painted a portrait of Mr. and Mrs. Jan Arnolfini. It's beautiful. It's also a wedding memento. Paintings commonly served as steps toward heaven (three saints, with kneeling donor) or secular instruction (Domenico di Bartolo's 1440 mural *Care of the Sick* on a wall of the leading hospital in Italy) or history lessons. The concept of high art—a.k.a. art with no work to do, a.k.a. art for art's sake—existed but was minor.

Northern Europeans are said to have changed that, and especially the English and Dutch. The change began with warships, which traditionally had been highly decorated. Beauty wins no battles, English and Dutch ship designers began to say. It does cost money. Sometimes it adds weight, too. Let's stick to powerful gunnery and efficient sailing and forget the carved sterns.

Actually, even without special decorations, square-rigged sailing ships are so beautiful that it was a long time before most people noticed the growing split between what is useful and what delights the eye. By the time they did, our culture was well down the road that leads to ugly factories behind ugly fences and then, some miles away, the (comparatively) attractive houses where the workers live. And also to pretty stone walls that fence nothing in or out—and hideous cyclone fencing that repels both intruders and the eye. At least on my farm, there is going to be no such split.

Something there is that loves a wall. That something is

called a human being. We build the Great Wall of China, curtain walls in castles, the Wailing Wall in Jerusalem, a thousand miles of stone wall in Connecticut, and we make the planet more beautiful than it was before. Now we just need to relearn what our ancestors knew—how to make that beauty part of the daily routine of ordinary life, the quotidian and the high casually mixed together.

1996

On Loan from the Sundance Sea

SCOTT RUSSELL SANDERS

WHY, YOU MAY ASK, DOES A WEATHER VANE IN THE shape of a fish swim atop the dome of the county courthouse in Bloomington, Indiana, six hundred miles from the sea? The explanations that circulate hereabouts range from sober to silly. A fish, some argue, simply has the right contour for a weather vane, long and flat to catch the wind. Some speculate that a few of the families who settled the town in 1818 may have migrated to the hills of southern Indiana from Massachusetts, where codfish whirled upon rooftops. Some think the weather vane is modeled on the perch in nearby ponds, even though it's the size of a ten-year-old child. Some explain the fish as a zoological compromise between Democrats, who wanted a rooster, and Republicans, who wanted an elephant. Some regard it as a symbol of Christ. Others see it as a warning that the actions of government, including those carried out in the courthouse below, may be fishy. Still others claim that the blacksmith who is given credit for hammering the weather vane out of a copper sheet and coating it with gold leaf in the 1820s actually brought it with him when he moved to Bloomington from Louisville, Kentucky, and therefore the fish hails not from an ocean or a pond but from a river, the mighty Ohio.

My own theory tends, I suppose, toward the crackpot end of the spectrum, but I will share it with you anyway, because it belongs to my private mythology of this place. I suspect that the courthouse fish swam up out of our ancestral memory, recalling the time when Indiana and the whole heart of the continent lay beneath a vast and shallow gulf, which geologists call the Sundance Sea. As the denizens of those inland waters died, their shells and bones settled to the bottom, forming a chalky mud that eventually hardened into limestone. Around a hundred million years ago, the heartland was raised above sea level by the erosion of the Appalachian and Allegheny Mountains, and Indiana has remained dry ever since. Although global warming may swell the oceans enough to flood coastal areas within the next hundred years or so, saltwater is unlikely to reach the heartland again anytime soon.

Meanwhile, I like to imagine that the fish atop the courthouse is keeping watch for the returning tide. Since I'm imagining, I think of it as a salmon—a coppery sockeye, maybe, overlaid with gold—spawned in a local stream and now seeking its way back to the deep. Whether salmon or codfish or perch, it's a token of wildness, reminding us that our land is on loan from the sea and that our own genes coil back through all our ancestors into those primordial waters.

WHEN FRIENDS WHO live on either coast ask me how I can bear to live in the hill country of southern Indiana, landlocked, high and dry, I tell them my home ground is not really so high, only about eight hundred feet above sea level, or so dry, because rain falls bountifully here and streams run through limestone caverns underfoot. Why, the place is so intimate with the sea, I tell them, that a salmon floats in our sky and our buildings rest on an old ocean floor.

Limestone is the ruling rock in this place. It's exposed in road cuts and creek beds. It dulls the blades of plows that scrape the thin topsoil. Bloomington is ringed by pits, where the buff or silvery stone is quarried, and by mills, where it is cut into elegant shapes. The foundations of the courthouse are laid on limestone; the building itself is fashioned out of it, as are many houses, banks, churches, and shops around town, as are tombstones in the cemeteries and monuments on the courthouse lawn.

I delight in knowing that much of my city is made from the husks of creatures that lived and died hundreds of millions of years ago in the Sundance Sea, just as I delight in knowing that our sun and solar system and the earth itself—the copper and gold of the weather vane, the calcium and carbon of your body and mine—are made from matter left behind by an earlier generation of stars. Although my city is more durable than my body, both are shaped out of recycled matter, both are caught up in the surf of decay and renewal, both are destined to survive for a spell and then yield their stuff to new constructions.

AT FIRST GLANCE nothing about the courthouse or the square that surrounds it, aside from that airborne fish, looks the least bit wild. The square is a patch in the latticework of streets laid out precisely north and south, east and west, part of the survey grid that stretches from the Ohio River to the Pacific. The Land Ordinance of 1785 provided for that survey as a way to reduce the unruly countryside into salable chunks. In America's interior there would be no more reckoning, as in the original colonies, by trees and boulders, rivers and hills; here the land would be sliced up into square sections as abstract as any geometrical proof. Today, a hawk spiraling over

Bloomington looks down on a checkerboard pattern softened only by a fuzz of trees.

At the center of that checkerboard, on a block of lawn dotted with war memorials, flagpoles, and Civil War cannons, rises the courthouse itself, some eight stories high, massive and imposing. The style of the building is a Beaux Arts mixture of classical elements—columns, pediments, balustrades, heroic statuary—capped by an octagonal drum and a mint-green dome. Ribbed like an old-fashioned football helmet and topped by curlicues worthy of a wedding cake, the dome gets its color, as the weather vane does, from the oxidation of copper. The whole affair is orderly, stately, solid, and symmetrical, proclaiming to all who care to look that here is the seat of government for a prosperous and law-abiding citizenry.

We're not always so law-abiding, of course, which is why we need courts and judges and jails. No sooner had the founders of Bloomington laid out the town in 1818 than they built a courthouse of logs. Made of timbers cut from nearby hills, it consisted of two rooms separated by a passageway and joined by a common roof—a style known appealingly as dogtrot. Each room had a single window facing east, to let in the morning light. A shelf in one of those rooms held the town's first library. The court met there in summer, the school in winter.

The new county, named Monroe in honor of the reigning president, soon outgrew the wooden dogtrot, and the commissioners ordered the construction of a larger courthouse, made from brick. The bricks were fired from a local deposit of clay, which was the off-scouring of rock from the Appalachians and Alleghenies. So the new courthouse, completed in 1826, was sheathed in a skin of baked mountain dust. Painted bright red with white trim, it soared from lime-stone foundations to a sharp steeple, up and up, until it culminated at the very tip in a weather vane shaped like a fish.

A man named Austin Seward either brought the copper fish with him when he moved to Bloomington around 1820 or else he fashioned it in his local blacksmith shop. Whichever the case, he affixed the weather vane to a post so that it hardly budged in the breeze, and therefore wasn't much good at nosing out the direction of the wind. Before long the gold leaf began to fray. When the county once again outgrew its courthouse, in the 1850s, the commissioners were inclined to retire the fish, but local voices rose in its defense. Given a new coating of gold by Seward's son, it was mounted on ball bearings to make it more responsive to the wind. Back up it went on the enlarged courthouse, and there it stayed for half a century, until the commissioners decided to replace the brick courthouse with an even larger one of limestone.

When the cornerstone for this grand edifice was laid in 1907, funds in the construction budget allowed not only for the finest limestone from local quarries but also for stained glass in the windows, murals in the rotunda, marble for the floors, cast iron for the balustrades, mahogany and oak for the railings and trim, brass for the lamps, and copper for the dome. But not one dime was available for repairing or re-mounting the battered weather vane. Once again an outcry arose. Civil War veterans raised funds to have the fish gilded anew and to have it installed in its rightful place atop the courthouse.

The limestone palace offered a public toilet and a room set aside where families could rendezvous when they came downtown. Friends would say, "I'll meet you under the fish." Enemies threatening lawsuits would say, "I'll talk to you under the fish." When folks came in from the countryside to do business in town, they often picnicked in the shade of the trees on the courthouse lawn, leaving crusts and rinds on the grass. The scraps attracted so many dogs and cats and flies that the same commissioners who had slighted the fish in their building plans now ordered the cutting down of the trees. This provoked another outcry, which led to the planting of oaks, maples, and sweet gums, which still comfort us nearly a century later.

THE LIMESTONE COURTHOUSE still presides over the city, but only because of the hard work and stubborn affection of many citizens. By the 1980s the interior had been carved up to provide additional offices and courtrooms; the furnace had become wheezy, the windows leaky, the pipes rusty, the wiring risky. When a grand jury, acting on advice of the fire marshal, threatened to close the building for safety violations, some commissioners called for tearing it down and putting up a sleek tower of glass and steel.

Yet again an outcry arose, this time in defense not merely of the fish but also of the grand old courthouse itself. By then I had been living in Bloomington for a decade; I had served on juries in the solemn building, had paid taxes there, had run my hands over its limestone flanks. I had come to see it as a symbol of our local landscape, quarried and shaped by local skills. I couldn't bear to think of a wrecking ball smashing the result of all that labor by carvers, sculptors, muralists, stained-glass artists, masons, and carpenters. I couldn't imagine the gilded weather vane swimming atop a steel tower, couldn't imagine wishing to run my hands over the flanks of a glassy box. So I added my voice to the uproar and my signature to the petitions for saving the courthouse.

Fortunately, there were many passionate defenders, including elders, students, businesspeople, and some elected officials. When the council met to decide whether to renovate or demolish, those in favor of preserving and restoring the courthouse prevailed by a single vote. I rejoiced, and it seems the whole community rejoiced, because the restoration of the courthouse and its weather vane, completed in 1984, set off a flurry of renovations downtown. A hotel, a creamery, and the Masonic lodge were turned into offices. A train depot was turned into a Japanese restaurant, a funeral home into condominiums, a warehouse into an antiques mall. A car showroom became a convention center, another a café. The old Carnegie Library became the county historical museum. The former city hall was transformed into an arts center, and a nearby cinema into a concert hall. A onetime furniture factory, complete with skylights set into a saw-toothed roof, now holds the city hall as well as lawyers' offices and high-tech businesses, and the adjacent parking lot now hosts the farmers' market. Thanks to the market, produce flows once more into the city from the countryside.

Many of the shops on the Courthouse Square have also been restored, and every single one is open for business. The old five-and-dime is now a bakery, the former hardware store now sells books, and the onetime department store holds a rug shop and a science museum for kids. Within sight of the courthouse you can find bars and banks, an adventure outfitter, a newsstand, a cooking-supplies shop, a photography studio, a recording studio, a furniture store, an ad agency, a Realtor, a grocery. You can park where the hitching racks used to be and stroll around the square to buy sporting goods, eyeglasses, musical recordings, hobby supplies, bicycles, clothes, jewelry, cigars, guitars, or paint. You can frater-

nize down there with the Moose, the Elks, the Masons, the
Knights of Pythias, or the Odd Fellows. One shop will sell
you the statue of a Union soldier brandishing a bayonet, another will sell you a wicker motorcycle, and another will sell
you a leopard-spotted brassiere. You can study yoga on the
square, plan a trip, frame a picture, play pool, eat cuisine
from Afghanistan or Ireland or Morocco, drink local or exotic
beers, have your fortune told by a clairvoyant, get a massage
or a manicure or a tattoo.

July Fourth parades, candlelight vigils, protest marches,
noontime concerts, political rallies—all focus on the courthouse. On Friday and Saturday nights teenagers cruise
around the square in pickup trucks and jalopies, or they park
nearby and sit on the hoods of their vehicles to gab. On summer weekends artists sell their wares from booths under the
shade of those courthouse trees. Near Christmas, musicians
dressed as Santa Claus show up on a fire engine to play carols on tubas, beneath a canopy of lights that stretches outward from the courthouse to the shops facing the square. In
spring, about the time the water is turned on in the Women's
Christian Temperance Union fountain, pink crab apples bloom
along the walkway leading up to the main door of the courthouse. If you go inside on a bright day and walk into the rotunda and look up, you will see a golden light shining through
stained glass, as if you were staring into the throat of a daf-
fodil.

The vitality in Bloomington's downtown swirls around that
green-domed, silver-flanked, statue-bedecked, fish-crowned
courthouse. This energy reminds us of why we gather into
communities to begin with. We come together to share gifts,
to practice our talents, to nurture and inspire one another. We
come together to build what we could not make separately.

Everywhere I look in the heart of my city, I see the handi-
work from past generations now carefully restored. I see the
results of our gathered powers. I see above all the courthouse, this expression not merely of our bedrock faith in civil
society but of our actual bedrock, lovely limestone, a cake of
past lives hardened on the floor of the Sundance Sea.

2001

A Fine Madness

JAN MORRIS

AS I WALKED NOT SO LONG AGO THROUGH THE BAB Zuweila in Cairo, below the dreadful objects of iron and chain that are, I take it, mementos of the time when this was the place of public executions, past the nail-studded gate behind which the long-dead levitating saint El Mutwalli attends the supplications of the faithful—as I entered the capital of the Fatimid caliphs, it occurred to me that the inner city, over which Western urban theorists wring their hands so helplessly, is decidedly alive and well in Egypt.

Al Qahira, "The Victorious," has not much changed its shape since it was founded in the tenth century. City walls surround part of its square mile or so, and it still feels quite separate from the vast metropolis that has grown up around it in successive centuries. It is a tumultuous jumble of tenements, bazaars, mosques, cramped squares, and narrow alleys: congested, crumbled, not very hygienic, with extremely poor housing and appalling pressures of traffic, noise, and general huggermuggerdom.

In short, our Western improvers would hate it. The health hazards! The safety hazards! The lack of zoning! The noise! The stress! The almost certain absence of qualified Counselors, Sociologists, and Planning Officers! But I think that within the medieval gates of this quarter one can discover almost all the qualities that an inner city ought to have—all but expunged in the West by the dogmatic reforms of experts.

I suspect the greatest of architectural visionaries, the Le Corbusiers or the Wrights, might be on my side. Like Venice, Al Qahira has an elegant simplicity of design that makes for clarity of purpose, too. It was conceived as a fortified palace compound: The palaces have vanished, but the rectangular ground plan remains much as it was when the caliph's Moroccan astrologers declared it propitious in 969 A.D.

Among the tangled maze of alleys a single main artery passes, with several changes of name. It runs from Bab Zuweila to Bab el Futuh, from the southern gate to the northern, following the line of an immemorial caravan route to the Red Sea. This was always the principal street of Grand Cairo, one of the great thoroughfares of the world, certainly one of the most resilient, and the true locale of the *Thousand and One Nights*—ostensibly set in Baghdad but really a reflection of this tremendous Oriental capital.

About halfway along stands the great bazaar quarter, Khan el Khalili, as magnetic a focus for tourists today as it was seven centuries ago for the turbaned merchants of the Eastern world—still gleaming with gold and silver, rich with carpets, sickly with perfumes, and cluttered with souvenirs ghastly and alluring. It forms a compact if labyrinthine quarter of its own: the medieval equivalent of a mall and the well-defined focus of commercial life in the city.

And nearby is the focus of intellectual and religious life—conterminous in medieval Islam, and to some degree in modern Islam, too. In a commanding situation more or less in the center of the place stands the great mosque-university of Al

Azhar, which has been for a thousand years the academic center of all Islam. Nowadays it has been vastly extended into an adjacent campus and into a campus outside the medieval city altogether, but it is still the symbolical and topographical apex of Al Qahira.

The form, then, is explicit: the one main highway linking every quarter with the centers of spiritual and temporal life, the whole contained within recognizable limits and given unity by the sanction of history. All around, in lanes and alleys and little squares, in buildings old and new, comfortable and appalling, the people of the city live.

Ah, the Western planners would say, but think of the squalor, the confusion, the jam-packed traffic of cars, trucks, buses, bicycles, donkeys, horses, herds of goats—men with baskets of ducks on their backs, street vendors, impertinent urchins, jolly smiling women, wandering mendicants—the rubbish, the crumbling walls, the piles of onions by the Bab el Futuh!

It is perfectly true that the moment you enter Bab Zuweila the full tide of human life overwhelms you with its torrent of flotsam and jetsam. Color, push, vivacity, greed, torpor, sudden anger, flirtation, reconciliation, resignation, humor—it is all there, all around you, out in the open. When I was walking here the other day I noticed a schoolboy, rucksack on his back, sauntering home through the streets, pausing sometimes to look in a shop or laugh at a traffic predicament, exchanging casual greetings all the way, meeting friends here and there, shooed away by stall keepers sometimes, eating a mandarin orange, dropping the peel, and carrying in his hand a plastic container containing a pair of large and vicious-looking insects. Far from thinking what squalors and perils surrounded him, I thought what a marvelous place it was to grow up in, with all the passionate variety of human existence displayed so intimately and so frankly, every step of the way.

The great Egyptian novelist Naguib Mahfouz did grow up here and in his most famous book, *Midaq Alley,* evoked a glorious cast of Al Qahiran characters—the rogues, the sentimentalists, the pious, the profane, the girl who ran away to be a downtown prostitute, the matchmaker, the quack, the man who made his living mutilating people to make their begging more profitable. His eponymous Midaq Alley still exists, in the heart of the place, and it pleased me to imagine that the schoolboy with his rucksack was a novelist in embryo, too, already soaking up his material.

For the first merit of this inner city is the scale of it. Nothing is too big; nothing is too far. The great central bazaar is there if you need it, but scattered throughout Al Qahira are food shops, street stalls, coffee shops, drapers—the Cairo equivalent of the corner shops whose disappearance in the West those town planners so deplore. Every few hundred yards there is a mosque or a shrine, too, binding Al Qahira in the loyalty of its faith and also providing a gentle place of escape, if the tumult of the street ever becomes too much for you.

The right scale and the right mix. Sacred and profane, exquisite and ruffianly, grand and poky—here all are cheek by jowl, with no inner ring roads to upset the ensemble or alienate one part from another.

One big modern road does strike into the city center, depositing its endless streams of traffic in the square outside Al Azhar, and no doubt much of Al Qahira's housing is really beyond redemption and will have to be replaced. No matter. What might ruin Al Qahira would be the application of trendy Western planning principles to its ancient web—the broadening of lanes, the opening up of spaces, the pedestrianization of that chaotic main street, which would at a single stroke destroy both the functionalism and the fascination of the place.

But short of mass demolition, even the most progressive reforms would probably fail in Al Qahira. For one thing, the cars and the donkeys would soon be back among the bollards and pretty benches of the pedestrian street. But much more importantly, the spirit of the place itself would prove indestructible. Al Qahira possesses one urban element that Western planners do not often have to bother about: the immensely potent force of a belief. Even patriotism, that last degraded form of religion, need not enter the calculations of town planners in the materialist West; but in Al Qahira the power of Islam in its most generous forms gives the whole place a public unity, and a practical form, too, that is beyond sociology.

Passing through Bab Zuweila is like entering the embrace of a family. God knows, as any reader of *Midaq Alley* certainly does, that the family has its fair share of family scandals and disgraces, its black sheep away in prison, its drug addicts, its lechers, and its snobs. But the children who grow up in Al Qahira grow up among friends, wandering in a city without fear, cheeky enough but innately polite, and infinitely better balanced, or so it seems to me, than children of our Western streets; and strangers, too, the moment they step into this ancient hubbub, feel themselves to be guests.

Life in all its complexity rages, laughs, plays, and asks for exorbitant prices on every corner of Al Qahira, but the grand and fundamental order that lies behind is betrayed in the neighborly pattern of the city, the courtesy of its streets, the tall and lovely minarets piercing the blue above; and that, to my mind, is what the inner city should be like.

1998

Building for the Ages

STEPHEN GOODWIN

I N MY SALAD DAYS, IN A FAR-OFF CORNER OF VIRGINIA, I BUILT a cabin. It was a modest cabin, only sixteen by eighteen feet, but in the chambers of my imagination it achieved majestic proportions. For me the sturdy little structure of log and stone was a monument, a triumph, a landmark, and—here is my small confession—I liked to think that in the fullness of time this spot, my spot, would become a destination for literary pilgrims. This was where I intended to write my books.

So I speak now of vanity, in particular the vanity of the young writer—or "junior author," as my pal the novelist Reynolds Price referred to me and my ilk from the lofty perch of his seniority. *Junior author.* That phrase neatly and wickedly expressed the gap between our ambition and our achievement. We were full of ourselves, I suppose, and set great store by our as yet unwritten works. This is the vanity of the junior author, this faith in the work that lies ahead, the belief that it matters more than anything else. Of course, it had better matter more than anything else or it will never get done. Vanity is the seductive voice that whispers in your ear, Write! Write! Write! That is what you were born to do.

First, though, I had to build the cabin. I expected that the building and writing would be more or less simultaneous, as they seemed to have been for Thoreau. As you have by now surely guessed, my true mentor was Thoreau and my holy book was *Walden*. The first essay I wrote about the cabin was called "Where We Live," and it gave homage to Thoreau. It was not lost on me that Thoreau's famous chapter "Where I Lived, and What I Lived For" is in the first person singular. He was an *isolato,* a poet, a naturalist, and a transcendentalist, while I was a married man, the father of a fine girl, and an aspiring novelist—in short, a familiar kind of young writer, who liked nothing better than to sit up half the night carousing and telling tales in the company of friends. Nevertheless, I thought my writing would flourish if I settled myself in a remote and virtuous place. I was going to live simply and write like a god. All I wanted was love, honor, riches, happiness, and immortality.

Like Thoreau, I also wanted and claimed for myself the joy of building. My first task was to gather stones for my foundation, and in no time I was stone smitten, ever on the lookout for stones of the right shape, hue, and texture, for stones of striking beauty and character. The trunk of my old Peugeot was usually full of stones I found along the country roads. It was slow work, but I was feeling patient, since I was building for the ages. I came to prefer the soft, tawny, golden sandstone that my mountain neighbors called fossil stone, and it was indeed stuccoed with the fossils of shellfish and mollusks. My foundation rose up from the earth, course by course, and it felt not merely solid, you understand, but ancient and prehistoric.

As for the logs, they went up in a twinkling. Most of them were already notched and hewn, for I took down and moved an old cabin. The logs were white pine and they were heartwood, but they did need some trimming, and a few of the topmost logs—the original cabin was two stories high—had rotted altogether. Tucked away somewhere I have photos of the junior author hard at work with his broadax. This old cabin also came with a large stone chimney, with fireplaces upstairs and down, and I have photos of the reconstructed chimney rising up like a rocket, with two proud young bucks standing, arms folded, on its pinnacle—the junior author and his brother.

We look mighty pleased with ourselves, which leads me to mention another sort of vanity—builder's vanity. Anyone who has ever built even the humblest structure has felt it. The mason who laid up the original chimney had left his initials and the date in one of the big blocks of sandstone: MFK 1877. And why shouldn't he sign it? An artist signs his work, and so does the builder, who knows that his work will outlast him. My brother's initials and mine are now scratched in the same stone.

Inside the cabin, my daughter's infant handprint is pressed into the mortar that chinks a space between the logs. Someday someone will trace that handprint with her own fingertips and dream a little dream about the child who used to play out by the hand pump and gaze up at her parents as they scuttled about in the scaffolding, building what must have looked to her like a castle in the air.

This someone will not really imagine my daughter, but never mind. A child's handprint is a powerful statement, a reminder of the single, specific, sweet, ceremonious, hopeful moment when a young couple held a child aloft and applied her hand firmly to the fresh mortar. We were just making a mark, leaving a sign of our passage, celebrating the fact that we had finally completed the chinking and closed the cabin against the weather and the critters.

We were entitled to stamp our identity on the cabin, I felt, since it was finished. That was builder's vanity, but as for my literary vanity—well, I hadn't finished much. The oeuvre was slender: a few short stories, a couple of essays. Now there could be no more delays, since my long writing table was installed along one wall of the cabin, and an engraving of Joseph Conrad watched sternly over this corner of the room. He looked wise, inscrutable, and dignified. He looked like an author.

I will refrain from telling you how much time the junior author spent wondering how he ought to look on his first book jacket. Yes, he did complete a novel, though little of it was actually written at the cabin, and kept all sorts of notes in his journals so that his biographer—so that posterity!—would know exactly how he had lived and worked. In his behalf, I should say that most of the writers I knew, junior and senior, were subject to these same reveries. We were all pursuing the white stag of fame, and we joked about elaborate measures to protect our manuscripts (in the freezer they would be safe from theft and fire). We wrote each other the kind of letters that made sense only if you imagined someone reading them a hundred years later. We told stories about each other as if we were already famous, or at least dead. And we visited the houses of writers and saw what intimate and sometimes random details of the writer's life came to be woven into their legend. I saw the creaking door in the house at Chawton, the door that signaled Jane Austen that someone was coming and she had better hide her writing from prying eyes. In Charlottesville I climbed the steps down which Faulkner drunkenly stumbled. At Key West I saw the kitchen where Hemingway had raised all the countertops because, the guide said with great relish, rolling his eyes theatrically, "Papa was a *big* man, and Papa had *big* appetites, and Papa caught *big* fish and cooked them right here!"

I never went so far as to imagine the kind of tour that would be given at my cabin, perhaps because I just couldn't figure out how the visitors were going to cross three mountain ranges and make their way down ten miles of twisting dirt road to find the place. But one winter I did settle in, and I wrote a second novel, and if I may, I would like to suggest this script for the tour:

> The winter of '77–'78 was bitter! During the day he cut wood and then he sat right here on those long winter nights, right here in this armchair. Look! The seat is like a death mask of his butt! He pulled the chair up as close as he could to the woodstove. He worked deep into the night, hearing nothing but the howling wind and the hiss of the burning logs. Then, to unwind, he'd take a nip or two of bourbon and go right out that door and stand on the porch, in the freezing cold, and sing fight songs. . . .

That is more or less how I remember that winter, anyway. The work was bracing and the stars were brilliant when I stepped out onto the porch. Now, as then, I take a detached view of the junior author: He was a different self, another me, and he seemed more interesting and possibly more important. He was certainly more extravagant. And he wrote a book that I still think is pretty good. I doubt that anyone is ever going to take the tour—and I haven't even mentioned the naked turkey hunt!—but I am grateful to have lived for a while in his element, where time and space seemed to radiate endlessly outward from that little cabin at the foot of a mountain.

That novel was the only book I wrote there. There have been other books of nonfiction, written elsewhere, for I felt the gravitational pull of the city. I held on to the cabin for years, though I went there less and less often. When I did go, I didn't have time to write; I spent my days there as a harried, cranky caretaker, never quite able to catch up with all the tasks that needed doing. Finally, ten years ago, I sold the cabin to a man who uses it as a hunting camp. He has put his own trophies on the walls. He is not after the white stag of fame but the white-tailed deer. For all I know he stands on the porch on starlit nights and sings hunting songs, creating his own myth and his own memories. I certainly hope so. We all need to celebrate our deeds, to set a value on them and raise them up high enough for safekeeping.

That is not vanity, not exactly, not unless we crow too much. In any case, the new owner is welcome to the cabin, for I have *my* cabin preserved in photographs, in a table made of cherry trees that grew on the mountainside, in thousands of words. "What thou lovest well remains," wrote Ezra Pound, "the rest is dross." I certainly loved that place and all that happened there, and I don't worry too much about the fierce old poet's warning: "Pull down thy vanity, I say pull down." Time will pull it down for us.

Time pulls down our vanity and makes preservationists of us all. Why else do we lug about our boxes of photographs, letters, clippings, and testimonials? And why do we treasure our grandfather's watch or our grandmother's garter, except that these objects somehow connect us to those we have loved? They live on in their belongings, and we who cherish them naturally wish for our own—let us not be afraid of the word—immortality.

Now that the cabin is someone else's, now that I am re-married and have a son as well as a daughter, now that I live in New York—in a house in an officially designated historic district—I sometimes wonder just what form my earthly immortality will take. I already know that this house will not bear my name; there is a plaque that calls it THE JAMES BATES HOUSE. I hope to write a few more books here, in a study cluttered with various dear possessions—a soccer ball signed by the members of a team I coached, a fabulous Mayan figure left to me by a friend who died ten years ago, my son's drawing of our furry dog, an engraving of a romantic tower that my wife gave me as a keepsake of our Irish honeymoon. There are books everywhere, but the only image of an author is a photograph of my great friend the short-story writer Peter Taylor, who was the best man at our wedding and present when our son was born.

In fact, as I look around my room, I see that I have surrounded myself, as we all do, with books and pictures and objects that are clues to what has mattered most, to the times when I have been happiest and most full of life. These belongings have only private meanings, but that is all they need to have. Or so I say, though even as I write these words, I am attempting to enlarge those meanings and make them more enduring.

Writers! They just can't help wanting things to last forever.

1997

The Vagaries of Memory

MAURICE ISSERMAN

NY PRIZE FOR THE BEST RETORT EVER DELIVERED AT Fort Ticonderoga, the great stone fortress that overlooks the falls linking Lakes George and Champlain in northern New York, would certainly go to Ethan Allen. Just before dawn on May 10, 1775, the Revolutionary War commander, with a company of Vermont Green Mountain Boys at his heels, stormed the gates of this strategically important British outpost, rousting its defenders from their barracks beds and taking them prisoner. One can imagine the emotions of the British officer who stared in amazement at Allen, a rough-hewn and intimidating presence even when he wasn't, as at present, brandishing a sword and swearing oaths against "damned British rats." The fort's commander, Captain William Delaplace, demanded to know by what authority were these rude strangers disturbing the slumber and security of His Majesty's forces. Allen thundered in reply, "In the name of the great Jehovah and the Continental Congress!"

A strong contender for the second-best rejoinder, in my opinion, was delivered two and a quarter centuries later, albeit under far less dramatic circumstances. I had spent an afternoon touring the fort with my two young children—Ruth, age nine, and David, age five. For them, both precocious history buffs, it was an enchanting first encounter; for me, a nostalgic return to a favorite childhood haunt I had not seen since the summers I had gone there with my own parents in the early 1960s. As we were leaving I mentioned to the museum ticket taker, a very pleasant young woman with whom I had chatted on our way in, that the fort seemed a lot smaller than I remembered. "You'd be surprised," she responded with a disarming smile, "how many middle-aged men say the exact same thing."

Afterward, in my middle-aged way, I reflected on the trip, and as I did so, other discrepancies surfaced between the way I remembered Ticonderoga from long ago and the way I encountered it upon return inspection. And it didn't seem to me that they could all simply be attributed to the vagaries and exaggerations of childhood memory. Where, for example, was the dungeon I recalled so vividly from earlier visits, a grimly thrilling tableau of uniformed mannequin inmates languishing under the fierce gaze of their mannequin jailer?

I decided to find out. At the invitation of Nicholas Westbrook, executive director of the Fort Ticonderoga Museum, I returned several months later for a closer look at the changes that had taken place in the institution since the 1960s. David accompanied me, wearing the tricornered hat and bearing the wooden musket he had acquired at the gift shop on our first trip. It was November, and the annual visiting season was at an end, but Westbrook took us around the grounds for a behind-the-scenes look at the fort's operation. It turned out that Ticonderoga did have a dungeon when I was a child. Indeed, it was such a popular feature with visitors that the fort's gift shop used to sell postcards depicting the inmates in their confinement. Unfortunately, there is absolutely no historical evidence that such a place actually existed some two hundred years earlier.

"Eighteenth-century armies in North America didn't imprison their wrongdoers," according to Westbrook, a friendly bearded man, who trained in early American history at the University of Pennsylvania and who made his first childhood visit to Fort Ticonderoga back around the same time I did. He too remembered the fort's dungeon exhibit, with what seemed a mixture of nostalgia and professional chagrin. The exhibit had been an artifact of a Ye Olde Tourist Trap mentality then prevailing at the fort and bore no relation to the actual nature of military discipline as practiced in colonial times. According to Westbrook, Ticonderoga's commanders simply "couldn't have spared the manpower" to fill a dungeon—either with languishing prisoners or with jailers. A soldier committing a heinous enough crime would have been executed; anything short of that would have met with swift punishment, a liberal application of the cat-o'-nine-tails on the unfortunate miscreant's bare back—after which he'd have been returned to the line.

So there's no dungeon at the fort today. Instead, visitors are invited to participate in the reenactment of actual courts-martial that took place in the eighteenth century for such offenses as drunkenness or going fishing without permission. After the evidence is presented and the victim has pleaded, participants get to vote on the verdict. (Authenticity has its limits, of course; good taste and occupational safety and health regulations spare the reenactors employed by the fort any actual acquaintance with the cat-o'-nine-tails.)

The dungeon's disappearance is emblematic of many of the changes that have taken place at Fort Ticonderoga in recent decades as romantic notions of the past have been swept away by a new vision of the site's significance, at once more austere imaginatively and yet richer historically than the one it replaced.

On the eve of the Seven Years War of 1756–1763, between the French and British colonial empires, French military engineers and laborers began constructing what they called Fort Carillon on a rocky ridge that commanded the heights above the lower reaches of Lake Champlain and the connecting outlet from Lake George. The fortress's location was carefully chosen. The French had a keen appreciation of North America's waterways, which made possible the empire's prosperity and security. At its northern terminus, Lake Champlain was connected via a tributary to the St. Lawrence River. From the lake's southern terminus, there was only a four-mile portage to Lake George, whose waters reached twenty-five miles farther southward into central New York.

The British swiftly recognized the threat posed by the new French fortifications to their own colonial interests; central New York and western New England would be at constant risk of attack from the French and their Native American allies so long as the fort remained in hostile hands. Beginning in 1757, the British and French engaged in a series of battles, culminating in the siege of Fort Carillon two years later. After the four-day-long attack, led by General Jeffrey Amherst, the British took possession of the fort.

For the next sixteen years, the British flag flew from the ramparts of what was now Fort Ticonderoga (which had been the Indian name for the region). Then Ethan Allen and the Green Mountain Boys showed up and secured the first military victory for the American revolutionaries. Fort Ticonderoga would change hands one last time, in 1777, when it fell to an invading British army commanded by General John

Burgoyne, who then marched south to defeat and surrender at Saratoga. The British and Hessian garrison he left behind at Ticonderoga abandoned the site upon learning of Burgoyne's disaster. Before departing, they set fire to its buildings, resulting in heavy damage. In a little over two decades the fort had been garrisoned by the armies of three nations, had been attacked on six separate occasions, and had fallen to attackers three times, but after the fire it would never again serve a military function.

Peace and decrepitude settled upon the old fortress. Local settlers hauled off stone from its crumbling walls and ruined barracks to provide the foundations for more pacifically intended dwellings. A century later, all that remained to remind passersby that this terrain was once fiercely contested were a few projecting piles of stone and masonry among high grass-covered mounds. Then a boy's imagination came into play. The fort and much of the surrounding landscape had been purchased early in the nineteenth century by a successful businessman named William Ferris Pell. In 1888 his great-grandson Stephen H. Pell, then eight years old, came upon an old bronze tinderbox beneath some loose stones. He treasured it as a memento of heroic days gone by and vowed then and there to someday restore the fort to its former glories. Twenty years later, having married well in the meantime and secured the necessary leisure and resources, Pell set out to realize his dream.

The old walls were uncovered, and a small army of workmen rebuilt them. In 1909, the Fort Ticonderoga Museum opened its doors to the public. President William Howard Taft and the French and British ambassadors were among those in attendance at the weeklong celebration of the fort's rebirth, which coincided with the three hundredth anniversary of the discovery of Lake Champlain by the French explorer Samuel de Champlain.

In the ninety years since, several million visitors have trod the grounds where Ethan Allen once held sway; in 1999 alone over a hundred thousand came. For most of that period, the fort remained a hobby for the family that ran it. In the museum's early decades, Pell was an active presence, personally conducting tours while turning away anyone he considered "inappropriately clothed" from the sacred precincts of the restored fort.

The spirit of Pell's amateur enthusiasms sometimes led the museum onto perilous interpretive ground (in the late 1950s, it dressed up mannequins, leading to a variety of suspect tableaux; in addition to the famous dungeon scene, there was also a highly improbable gathering of French soldiers toasting one another with bottles of wine in what seemed to be a rustic cabaret). But Westbrook, who has been director of the museum since 1989, gives Pell credit for breaking new ground in the field of historical restoration. From the beginning, Fort Ticonderoga was more than just a scenic replica. The many artifacts dug up on its grounds were carefully preserved and lovingly displayed in the museum's galleries, including nearly a thousand muskets, pistols, swords, and other eighteenth-century weapons. In 1927, Pell launched a scholarly journal, *The Bulletin of the Fort Ticonderoga Museum,* which performed pioneering work in the integration of the study of material culture with documentary history. And he provided the makings of a great library of colonial military history, the fruits of which can be found in the books and manuscript collections gathered in the Thompson-Pell Research Center, opened just outside the grounds of the fort in 1992.

Today the museum is run by the not-for-profit Fort Ticonderoga Association. The fort is open to visitors from early May through late October, and in addition to its permanent exhibits, there are daily performances in July and August by a resident fife-and-drum corps, artillery and firearm demonstrations, and the like. French and Indian War reenactors descend here annually in late June, as do Revolutionary War reenactors in mid-September. The fort's guides, and the interpretive panels on its grounds, emphasize that the story of Ticonderoga is one that was lived by both Native and European Americans, and by women as well as men. A great deal of attention is paid to the surrounding landscape; over the years the fort has acquired two thousand acres of land for its own grounds and, even more important, has bought up development rights for much of the land visible from the fort, on both the New York and Vermont sides of Lake Champlain. If the surrounding open fields bear little resemblance to the wooded hillsides of the eighteenth century, at least the fort has done well in keeping the twentieth century at bay.

As Westbrook walked us around the grounds of the fort in November, he often had to raise his voice to compete with the roar of construction; David was almost as interested this time in watching the earthmovers as he was in playing with the cannon. For all of its imposing presence, the fort is a fragile artifact. A constant battle is fought to keep the place from falling down; water seeping into the rubble fill of the ten-foot-thick walls has done more damage than was ever wreaked by enemy artillery. In 1997 the outer walls of the western demilune (a semidetached bastion) collapsed, fortunately during the off-season. In 1998 the fort undertook an ambitious five-year plan to shore up all the walls and gun decks. At the same time, the never-restored east barracks will be rebuilt as an education and exhibition center. By the time the museum's centennial rolls around, in 2009, it plans to be offering year-round educational programs.

As a historian, I appreciate the changes that recent years have brought to the fort. The past may be past, but it's not static. The story necessarily changes as we learn to ask new questions and discard outworn assumptions. I know all that. I accept its inevitability. Still, I have to confess, there's a part of me that misses that stupid dungeon. It is, alas, an authentic part of my own history, if not the fort's.

I remember a ten-year-old boy standing on the ramparts of Fort Ticonderoga on a sunny summer day in 1961. He manned a weathered cannon many times his size and squinted down its barrel at onrushing enemy hordes. (They were, oddly enough, Mexicans attacking the Alamo; he wasn't a stickler for historical accuracy—besides, he had his Davy Crockett hat on.) Like all his brave countrymen, he was the kind of boy who would never retreat in the face of desperate odds, never flinch, never shirk, never doubt. I liked that boy. Sometimes over the years I wondered what happened to him. I was glad to catch a glimpse of him the other day at Fort Ticonderoga.

2000

Something Fishy
in Small Town X

WAYNE CURTIS

ONE AFTERNOON LAST FEBRUARY A LATE-MODEL Volvo rolled to a stop just outside my house, its engine dead. The driver got out, opened the hood, and peered underneath. I was upstairs catching up on e-mail at the time, but I immediately put on my glasses and canted toward the window to get a better view. Those of us who live in small towns rarely admit to it, but things like a stalled car in front of one's house can make the difference between a dull day and an eventful one.

The driver spent a minute or two poking at wires, then turned and strode off down the block. A few minutes later he returned in a white cargo van driven by someone else, and the two men began busying themselves with jumper cables. They were both in their late twenties and wore shiny winter parkas, and neither they nor their vehicles looked familiar to me. It was all very strange. I moved closer to the window and stared, as if a pair of crested auklets had suddenly alighted on our yard.

Then a lightbulb went on: Those rumors? They had to be true. In recent weeks reports had circulated around Eastport, the remote coastal Maine town where I've lived for the past three years, that a California outfit was coming here to make a movie or TV pilot or some such thing. I didn't pay much attention. Eastport is as far as you can be from Hollywood and still be in the continental United States, so talk of moviemaking seemed more than a little far-fetched.

Yet just outside my window these interesting harbingers suddenly appeared. The Volvo soon started up, and this pair drove off, but within a couple of weeks a flock of others descended upon the town—carpenters, sign painters, telephone installers, sound technicians, theatrical-lighting specialists, and a large number of artisans, the last of whom occupied a disused lumberyard at the edge of town and converted it into a sophisticated operation for the production of props and other objects. Around town were also seen knots of young people whose function was not immediately apparent but who carried clipboards and walked with that oversized sense of purpose that carrying a clipboard always imparts.

What precisely the Hollywood people were up to was all rather hush-hush; local workers were required to sign exhaustive nondisclosure forms, and the clipboard people would only hint at a documentary-style murder mystery. It wasn't until some weeks later that we learned what was up—the crew was here to shoot a new reality TV show for Fox Television called *Murder in Small Town X*. The show aired this past summer and fall, just a few months after filming concluded.

The program involved ten real-life contestants who sought to solve a series of "murders" in a strange and quirky village ("a make-believe small town," *The Wall Street Journal* reported) without being "killed" themselves. Several hundred townspeople were hired to more or less play themselves, and actors mingled among them. This show was described as *Survivor* meets *Twin Peaks*.

But the mix of real and fake was equally perplexing to those of us who lived in Eastport as it transmogrified last spring from a near ghost town to a bustling mini-metropolis. Each day it became harder to recognize the place under all its pancake makeup. After decades of being so far out of the picture as to not even be in the theater, our town was at last ready for its close-up.

Eastport is about a seven-hour drive northeast of Boston, much of that through tracts of timberland on narrow roads crumbling along the margins. It's the easternmost city in the United States, and from downtown one looks across the blue-gray waters of Passamaquoddy Bay to a disjointed archipelago of spruce-covered islands, all of which are in Canada. The bay was once the heart of the eastern sardine industry, and in 1880 Eastport had eighteen canneries and five thousand residents. Islanders with shopping lists in hand once streamed by ferry into town, one of the bay's major mercantile hubs.

Our two-block-long waterfront downtown, which dates from that turn-of-the-century heyday, is lined with handsome two- and three-story storefronts of brick and cast iron. As in many coastal cities, our main street is called Water Street, and it wraps around a gentle bend as it follows the harbor's edge. The downtown is bracketed at either end—by a granite-faced post office with a tower at one end and a tall, vaguely Gothic brick building that used to be a bank on the other. This configuration makes Water Street feel like a comfortably enclosed space, a cozy living room just off the squinty expansiveness of the bay.

Most of the downtown architecture displays a sort of frontier enthusiasm, a giddy boomtown exuberance, with elaborate cornices and oddly bulbous protuberances on many pilasters. Nineteenth-century Eastporters must have surmised that good times at the far rim of the country were likely to be fleeting, so why not really enjoy them?

They were right. To my knowledge, the word *giddy* has not been used to describe the town in recent years. Eastport's current economic condition is at least partly related to the number of sardines you've eaten lately, which I'm pretty sure is none. This proto–fast food item has fallen out of fashion over the past few decades; the town's last sardine cannery was shuttered in 1983. Ferries to the islands have been reduced to a seasonal curiosity, and the retail trade decamped thirty-five minutes north to the town of Calais, where Wal-Mart opened a store a few years ago. The town's population has dwindled, at last count, to sixteen hundred.

The erosion in both population and the retail trade has resulted in a predictable imbalance between the supply of old buildings and the demand for them. Although Eastport can claim several superlatives in addition to being America's easternmost city—it's the foggiest city on the East Coast, for example, and it's home to the largest tidal whirlpool in the Western Hemisphere—it's perhaps most famous for the melancholy emptiness of its downtown.

From time to time bemused tourists will stop residents and ask, "What happened here?"—as if the town had suffered some cataclysmic event, perhaps a meteor strike. Though the downtown does still have a handful of active businesses (there's a fine old hardware shop, a variety store, and three restaurants), Eastport is a husk of its former self. At times it can look like an ailing farm town from the Dakotas that came to the seashore for recuperation and stayed. Instead of tumbleweeds, Eastport has dense, silvery fogs that sheathe stationary objects with evanescent halos. It's really quite beautiful, and at night I like to admire the town while walking my dog down the middle of Water Street, which is something I can usually do without endangering either of us.

THEN HOLLYWOOD CAME to town with its clipboards and rented white vans. In the arithmetic of the entertainment economy, empty and interesting buildings are apparently a valuable resource, much the way schools of herring once were to the old economy. "We drove in, looked at it for five minutes, then basically booked it," Leslie Radakovitch, the supervising producer of the Fox show, told me. "The town is like a standing back lot. It's hard to get a bad shot here."

Raw space you can find on a soundstage, of course. Eastport had more—a distinctiveness and authenticity, that ineffable small-town flavor that could be conveyed on the small screen in a few selective shots. "It's so unique here," Radakovitch said. "Downtown is so untouched, and you always want to bring a fresh vision to what you're doing."

One can normally be confident that the street one leaves in the morning will look the same when one returns home that night. That wasn't so in Eastport this spring. It was as if two decades had passed in the course of two weeks. The production team rented every vacant storefront on Water Street, along with a number of other sites around town: a Victorian house, an old barn, a decrepit house on a point. The plywood came down off empty Water Street windows, and Potemkin shops appeared daily. New signs flourished—for Scrodbury's Barber Shop, Crabby Carl's TV Repair Shop, a Nokia phone dealer (product placement was big in this series), and a candy shop. Dusty display windows where cobwebs had clung unmolested for years were cleaned and repainted, then filled with TVs and cotton candy and pottery.

A few storefronts became actual settings for "investigators" to visit in search of clues. There was a trendy nightclub with a huge clamshell back bar called the Sunset Club, and Sparky's Museum of Taxidermied Wonders, which featured a bedraggled lion peering from the window and a sign bearing the face of a too-happy clown. (What's a TV murder mystery without a clown?) A twelve-foot-tall statue of a lushly bearded fisherman toting a cod was installed one afternoon at the head of the fishing pier. It all made for a nice town, if a somewhat peculiar one.

Eastport was renamed Sunrise, and new signs cropped up everywhere—on city hall, on the sporty new police cars that raced around the streets, on a new downtown billboard. Even the WELCOME TO EASTPORT sign at the edge of town was covered over. The local paper reported that at least one pair of baffled travelers was spotted trying to figure out where Sunrise was on a road map.

Once the shooting began in earnest in early April, life in Eastport became even more disorienting. A car careened off a pier, stretch limos with tinted windows crept through town, a fishing boat blew up just off the breakwater. Posters inquiring after a missing family were tacked up around town one day, and I caught myself looking to see if anyone in the photo seemed familiar. The new town's sly insinuation into my life became clear the day I absentmindedly read a newspaper story about Nokia's quarterly earnings—in my life I have never once read an article about corporate earnings—somehow believing the results had local impact.

Most of the production people I saw around town often communicated with two-way radios, so I dug an old Radio Shack scanner out of a closet. For several weeks, the scanner crackled to life constantly while I was dubbing around the yard or cooking dinner or even working at my desk. (My fiancée made clear to me that leaving it on the bedside table at night—even with the volume down low—was not acceptable behavior.) The radio allowed me to tap into the rich aquifer of small dramas taking place around town. "What should we do with the bagpipe lady?" "Could somebody please find me a scary-looking letter opener?" "Who has the severed fingers to go into the can?" It was all quite fascinating to me. When the scanner was turned off, life outside my window didn't seem nearly as interesting or sensible; it was like watching television without the audio, both dull and uninformative.

HOLLYWOOD GOT AN empty downtown with a surfeit of distinctiveness and charm. What did Eastport get out of the deal?

Besides the obvious—scads of cash, which Hollywood dispensed from seemingly inexhaustible checking accounts—we got an actual bustling town, not just a faux one. The storefronts may have been a scrim, but all that activity in front of them was real, and it had a multiplier effect. As word got out about the filming, people trekked to Eastport from all over the region. The town offered proof of William Whyte's dictum that people attract other people. With the influx of Californians and others, Eastporters suddenly seemed to be out and about in great numbers. From my desk each afternoon, I watched a steady stream of families and teenagers and elderly folks walk downtown to see what was going on.

The most extraordinary transformation was at night. Before, downtown was almost always empty and dimly lit after dark; it usually had the murky feel of an aquarium filled with algae. But now the fake shops were all ablaze from within, and the high-wattage stage lights dressed up the building fronts (even the two tugboats tied up at the fish pier were lit up), so the town had a preternatural liveliness to it. Filming often ran late into the night, and even on quiet nights, when people weren't scurrying about, security guards sat in dark parked cars you could identify by the diodelike orange glow of cigarettes inside. Late one night after an April snowstorm I walked downtown, and the computers in the production office and the Nokia sign and the televisions in Crabby Carl's all spilled a lovely blue light out onto the freshly fallen snow, making the town seem for a moment very much part of the present century.

Even more than money and activity, the production validated the town in a curiously modern way. The geography I learned in school was always a matter of physical absolutes. Eastport, for example, merits a dot precisely this large on the map, since such dots are reserved for towns between one thousand and five thousand inhabitants.

But there's a parallel geography for a small town, an invisible topography, if that town has made it into film or television or even a commercial: It merits a bigger dot on this other map. The town becomes known, and when you describe it to people farther afield, their eyebrows rise in acknowledgment—"Hey, I saw that place in that Harrison Ford movie!"— even if its name isn't immediately familiar. The parallel cultural geography isn't new. It merely replaces an older one. Small towns once acquired bigger dots on the map by building handsome libraries or town parks designed after the contemporary fashion or theaters where the B-list vaudevillians occasionally performed. These features, in turn, replaced natural wonders like stone arches or mossy chasms or cliffs that from certain angles vaguely resembled the profile of an Indian princess. (Eastport's tidal whirlpool was once an attraction but is now largely ignored.)

You can find traces of this other geography in every small town where Hollywood has even briefly alighted. Curling photos of movie stars are tacked to the wall next to restaurant cash registers, and yellowing local newspaper stories about past productions occupy drawers in houses throughout town. If you bring the subject up, you'll get animated stories from even taciturn residents—about that time Randy Quaid sat right on that diner stool you're sitting on now, about that time Geena Davis walked right by as close as I am to you, only she was smaller than you would have thought.

During the production of *Murder in Small Town X,* I e-mailed a friend about it, and she responded, yeah, well, we had a real movie made in our town this winter, one with Susan Sarandon. I felt trumped. They had a bigger dot on the cultural map.

Production crews leave their own topographic landmarks, of course. In Townshend, Vermont, there's a handsome bandstand on the green, different from other New England bandstands in that it was constructed for a Chevy Chase movie some years back. In a used-car lot in Rockland, Maine, I once saw a 1963 Chevy Bel Air with a dashboard signed by Mel Gibson and windows smudged from all the noses that had pressed up against it.

When the filming concluded in Eastport, the producers donated the statue of the cod fisherman to the town. During production and all through the summer, travelers stopped by to have their snapshots taken in front of the big fellow with the cod. Eventually the fiberglass and foam will start to delaminate and look tatty; ten or fifteen years from now the city council will probably convene to discuss hauling the statue off to the dump. But until then, it's our pushpin on the new map. This is where we are.

. . .

THE FILMING CONCLUDED on May 12 with a parade through town. Eastporters were all invited, and large signs bearing the words CONSENT TO BEING PHOTOGRAPHED appeared on makeshift barricades set up on every street leading downtown. The fictionalized parade (not unlike the actual one Eastport holds every Fourth of July) had high school bands and veterans carrying flags and vintage cars and a float or two and a smattering of cute toddlers waving banners. An actor played our police chief; our actual city manager played himself. Stock characters we had gotten used to seeing around town—unsmiling street sweepers dressed in somber black suits—took part as well.

I walked down the block from my house and stood on the curb where a production assistant told me to stand. I waved to the floats when the director told us to wave, and if you don't mind my saying so, I believe I brought an uncommon depth to my role as a small-town resident. The parade circled around Water Street twice, then the director said, "Cut!" through his bullhorn, and just like that it was over.

The members of the production crew hugged each other and scrambled into vans. The whole town was beset with a melancholy air, like a college campus the day after graduation.

Over the next few days, Sunrise was loaded up into a stream of Ryder trucks that headed west. First went the signs for the new shops, then the stuff in the windows, leaving many storefronts vacant and hollow-eyed once again. The more garish trim colors were painted over, and the fleet of rental cars and vans that had clogged our streets diminished, then disappeared. Only the statue of the cod fisherman and a bus-stop sign remained as evidence that anything unusual had happened here.

These days the town is quiet and largely empty. I sit at my desk upstairs in my house, quite undistracted, since hardly anybody walks past, even on sunny summer afternoons. From time to time, I'll turn on the scanner on my desk to see what's going on, but mostly I'm greeted with a staticky hiss. Once in a while, though, the emptiness is broken by a police officer calling in the license number of someone headed out of town and driving too fast.

And that makes for a somewhat eventful day.

2001

The Sensation
of Infinity

ANITA DESAI

WHY MEXICO? I AM CONSTANTLY ASKED AND, PACK-
ing up my bags to leave the gray, frozen, colorless north, I am
as puzzled by the question as people are by the regularity
with which I leave for Mexico.

To me, the very name spells everything attractive and enchanting: an ancient name of a land where every stone and
rock is old, old and imbued with history, where vistas are
endless and the light is so pure it dazzles, like crystal, or
flame. Who would not want to leave the dullness of the
north, this rawness and sad urban ugliness, for a land where
volcanoes rise from the valleys into snow-topped cones,
where hills flow outward in waves of lilac and rose and violet all the way up to the horizon, where trees bear golden or-
anges and lemons as in some romantic ballad and flowers
bloom in colors so rich and varied as are not dreamt of in the
north?

That is the obvious answer, it seems to me, but since no
one I have tried to explain this to seems in the least convinced, I have to go further and admit that of course there is
more than the attraction of a perfect climate—the eternal
spring that Cortés and the *conquistadores* discovered—or of

beautiful scenery and marvelous food for one who spends the workaday life in a northern city, catching a bus and descending into the subway to go to work, returning after dark through streets where no life stirs except for the automobiles hurrying by.

WHEN I GIVE the matter thought (and usually it is a matter of instinct rather than thought), then I realize that being Indian has something to do with the affinity I feel with the land about which I knew nothing till, one bitter New England winter, I could not bear the cold or the dark another day and simply packed my bag and flew to Oaxaca, and on landing at the little airport surrounded by low scrubby hills and flowering bougainvillea and flooded with a light of piercing clarity, I felt like the surrealist André Breton, who said: "I dreamt of Mexico and I am in Mexico. . . . Never before has reality fulfilled with such splendour the promises of dreams." After checking into a hotel, I walked out of the tropical jungle contained in its courtyard, with cages full of squawking parrots, and found a church built of stone, a jacaranda tree blooming against the cobalt sky, and children playing with a ball in the dust and felt an urge, unknown to me before, to go down on my knees and kiss those stones, that dust. Clearly, I had had the experience, albeit in reverse, that Octavio Paz described in *In Light of India* when he wrote, "The strangeness of India brought to mind another strangeness: my own country."

I have visited and loved many places in the world, places I am always happy to see again and of which I have dear memories, but my response to Mexico goes much deeper and was formed much faster—in fact, instantly. I have to put this down to an affinity of the blood, an affinity of race and tribe that I would not normally acknowledge. I have not seriously

explored the prehistoric link between the Indians of India
and the Indians of the Americas, but I do know it must exist,
because when I am in Mexico, I do not feel a stranger, nor am
I regarded as one. I feel I know and understand this place
without having to have it explained to me. In the north, when
I walk down a street and catch glimpses of the lives lived in
the closed houses I pass, I am filled with the desolation of
finding the streetscape utterly foreign to me, of not knowing
what goes on behind the picture windows and the white
picket fences, whereas in Mexico, when I see a crowd waiting at a bus stop or clustered around a barrow of food, or
when I see a family strolling through a park or old women
climbing stairs to a cathedral to light candles there, I know instinctively what they are thinking, what they are talking
about, why and how. There is no sense of strangeness, of in-
scrutability—it is as though I have lived there always.

In a way, I have: India is so similar, the way of life so familiar. Oh, there are obvious differences: Mexicans were all
converted to Christianity, Indians were not; Mexicans ac-
cepted Spanish ways far more than Indians did British—but,
just as in India, one has a constant awareness in Mexico of
history being a palimpsest, with layers and layers of time ac-
creting to form the present, each contributing to what life is
now. This is the great contrast with the civilizations of the
north, where what you see on the surface is what there is
beneath. Here, too, is a culture that is not monolithic and un-
divided but, on the contrary, diverse and manifold. Kaleido-
scopically, it is forever presenting different views, different
patterns.

There are differences, certainly: The quietness, the silence,
of the Mexican is certainly not shared by the Indian. Travelers from D. H. Lawrence to Graham Greene to Sybille Bed-

ford have commented on the ability of the Mexican to remain still, silent, isolated even in a crowd. They have interpreted it as sullenness, stupidity, or danger; I see it differently—as a well of thought that goes down, down deep into history and long experience, reaching to the very heart of things, to an Indian self buried beneath all the centuries of otherness. Very few Indians from India are capable of such silence, such isolation—it has to be acquired and cultivated. Whereas Mexicans escape from it into the cacophony of music, fireworks, and the drunkenness of fiestas with exhausting, even tiresome, frequency, in India, one feels the need to escape from the press of people into solitude, as in meditation.

ON MY VISITS to Mexico, I find myself returning to two towns over and over, and they stand in sharp contrast to each other. In certain moods I am drawn to one, in others I am drawn to the other.

One is San Miguel de Allende, a sixteenth-century Spanish colonial town high in the mountains of the Sierra Madre Occidental to the northwest of Mexico City. Climatically speaking, it is "high desert," a zone I had not encountered before: The Himalayan mountains I know are wooded and lush. Here the mountains are sere, with very little growth, low and scrubby, and it is where I discovered how beautiful earth and rock are in themselves, how varied at different times of day: "Untiring games of light, always different and always the same," Octavio Paz wrote, give "the sensation of infinity and pacify the soul." The light is pale, almost opalescent, in the early morning, dun and ochre in the blaze of afternoon, before acquiring violet and rose and indigo tints as the sun sinks over the valley and disappears behind the farthest rim of hills.

The houses are built of the soft pink stone of the region

that the desert light turns to rose. All day, bells ring from one
cathedral or another, striking the hours and pealing to celebrate a particular occasion. Old women wrapped in shawls
climb the stairs with bouquets as tall as themselves of white
calla lilies and bloodred gladioli to offer to the gilt images
glowing in the flickering candlelight inside. Often the women
are accompanied by small children, who continue to play
among the pews as they might outside; often even a dog will
sink down on the cool stone floor for a little nap, or a young
couple, holding hands, will drop in to make a sign of the
cross before going out into the sunshine to find themselves
an ice cream.

The entire town is given over to the leisurely stroll, and
most strolls end up in the little *jardín,* or central plaza, in
front of the great pink stone cake of the *parroquia,* the parish
church. Low, bushy trees cast an intense shade on the hottest
days over the benches where everyone gathers to wait for the
day's newspapers to arrive, get their shoes shined to a high
gloss, watch children chasing the plump pigeons around, listen to a mariachi band play, and, of course, snack on roasted
corn on the cob or ice cream in a hundred flavors, from
tequila to tamarind. This is a town where no one wakes to an
alarm clock, no one runs; the sun imposes its slow, stately
measure, and the body gratefully accepts it. Here one realizes
that a city can mold itself to its environment; it need not op-
pose or destroy its surroundings, as elsewhere.

Pleasant as the *jardín* is in the day, at night it is magical—
lamps bloom into light, the daytime bustle disappears like
one act of a play giving way to the next, and, on the steps of
the *parroquia,* the *estudiantinas* of the local university
gather, dressed in the costume of medieval troubadours—
flowing black capes and colored ribbons, velvet caps and

buckled shoes. They come with their guitars and tambourines to sing old Spanish ballads. When a ring of listeners has gathered—and they tend to be Mexicans, not foreign tourists—the *estudiantinas* lead them up and down the cobbled streets, singing; a little burro trots alongside, carrying a cask of wine to help create the illusion of a medieval and romantic Spanish city under the burning Mexican stars.

Day and night, dark and light. When morning dawns, white egrets rise from the trees in the Parque Juárez, soaring up into the radiant bubble of the sky and drifting away for the day. As evening approaches, they return, descending into the trees where they nest in the spring and raise their fledglings in the summer before migrating for the winter. At the same hour, all the black, glossy grackles settle for the night in great hordes in the trees around the *jardín* with the greatest possible avian cacophony. It might be a chess game played out in the sky by white bird, black bird, changing day for night.

TO AN EVEN greater extent is one aware of the place of the human being in the natural world in a little town, a village really, to the south of Mexico City and northeast of Cuernavaca, a place called Tepoztlán, nestled against the forested flanks of hills and spilling into the valley below. Although the houses look recent and temporary compared to those of the Spanish colonial towns to the north—really little more than constructions of the local black lava stone or of adobe bricks under sloping tiled roofs—it is actually a far, far older habitation. There are people here who speak no Spanish but only Nahuatl, and the steep roads were laid in pre-Columbian times, according to the design of the Aztec pyramid temple— a steep incline with a level platform, then another steep incline and another level platform, and so on till one reaches the top. At the highest peak, twelve hundred feet above the valley, stands the temple of El Tepozteco, the god of harvest, fertility, and wine, whose festival is celebrated with much dance and drink for three days in the spring (the Dominican friars who brought Christianity to the place found it impossible to dislodge this cult and fabricated a Christian festival to coincide with it, so its rites are conducted within the boundaries of the cathedral grounds). The converts embraced the Christian faith with that inclusiveness so much a mark of Mexican culture, and each of the seven *barrios* of the town—named after the bird, insect, or reptile most common to that area: scorpion, lizard, turtle, for example—has its own church and its own saint, who is venerated with three-day festivals twice a year. As a result, the whole year round, the town resounds with music, dances, and, most deafeningly, fireworks—built into towering *castillos*—that are set off at sunset. On these occasions every house in the *barrio* will open its doors so neighbors and strangers may enter, seat themselves at the long tables laid under the avocado and custard apple trees, and share the food (papayas and mangoes carved into elaborate flowers on sticks, ice cream, tamales, corn on the cob, chili sauce) and hospitality.

Then there is the open market, held twice a week, to which people from surrounding villages have brought their produce and crafts for generations and centuries—fruit and vegetables, grains and spices on Wednesday; arts and crafts (baskets, gourds, pottery, silver, and copperware) on Sunday. If a pig has been slaughtered, its head will be mounted outside; if a goat, then the goat's. As in India, no attempt is made to disguise or obscure.

The Convento Domínico de la Natividad is the still center of all the town's festivities and commerce, its quiet cloisters painted with fading red roses, its refectory with the figures of the Dominican friars who first occupied cells on the upper floor, which have some of the fairest views in all Mexico. Nowadays these rooms house a museum of local lore and galleries that display the work of local and visiting artists.

But one has only to walk a little way down the steep roads radiating from the center to see that the town is little more than a marketplace; most people still live as if they were in the country, their walled compounds guarded by packs of dogs and full of chickens, turkeys, woodpiles, washing troughs, and the coffee bushes that provide the red berries one can smell being roasted over fires and ground early in the morning. In no time at all one is out in the countryside, and the ranches and haciendas of the rich from Cuernavaca and Mexico City give way to the cornfields, orchards, streams, and forests that have always been there. The roads here are made for horses, burros, and sandaled feet, not automobiles. At dusk one sees shepherds leading their flocks home and farmers carrying machetes back from their fields, and then the land is swallowed up by the dark. The night has enormous depth, and the night sky brilliance; one is very aware that this land gave birth to the legendary Aztec serpent god, Quetzalcoatl. Perhaps it is why artists and writers have always come here—to find the pulse of that creative force.

Perhaps. Perhaps not. What does make Mexico, for me, the perfect environment for a writer is that slow, regular heartbeat of time in a land where it has been beating for a long, long time, through so much history, building up a long, long past into which one may immerse oneself, then reemerge—the same, yet altered, renewed. In the same spirit of contradiction, one can be solitary as a writer must be solitary, on a patio or a veranda with one's books and papers, but whereas in the city this solitude is confining, deadening, here in a Mexican village one is never truly isolated or separated. Birds as tiny as butterflies come by to sip from the flowers around one, butterflies as large as birds swoop regally by, and all around there is the hum of life: the village dogs exchanging threats and insults, the church bells booming, the vendor going by with his bucket of boiled corncobs, the knife sharpener on his bicycle who plays but two melancholy notes on his little pipe, the maid sluicing down the paving stones of the patio or thrashing clothes in the trough, a burro trotting by with a load of firewood, a fountain trickling (and, yes, one must admit, at least six radios blaring in the compounds around) . . . One is not banished from the web of life, one is included. A metaphor, is that not, for art?

2002

The Best Big Room

MALCOLM JONES

I HAVE BEEN GOING THROUGH GRAND CENTRAL TERMINAL IN New York City for twenty years, and I can't get enough of it. The first time I went, I was an out-of-towner. It was my first trip to New York, and Grand Central was just something I thought I should see, because it was one of those places that I'd heard people talking about all my life. I spent most of a Saturday morning prowling around the terminal. Eventually, I found myself in a corner stairwell. There was no one around to stop me, so up I went. On the fifth-floor landing I found an unlocked door and entered. I was in a passageway made almost entirely of glass. On either side of me were banks of windows about five feet apart, and a catwalk ran between them for about fifty feet.

I had stumbled into one of the building's engineering marvels, the double wall of windows at the east and west ends of the main concourse, which can be regulated to control the big room's temperature. It is a marvel of function, but it is also a sight to see. Right above me, almost close enough to touch, was the famous sky ceiling. Below, people moved across the floor like something seen under a slide. I don't know how long I stayed up there in my angelic tree house, probably only a few minutes, but the sense of elation I felt was like a shot of pure oxygen. For the first and only time in my life, I felt a little godlike, as though the whole building belonged to me and those people 125 feet down below on my Tennessee marble floor were merely there at my whim. I left before I got thrown out, but I left reluctantly. And I couldn't wait to go back.

I returned every chance I got. Once in a while I even went to catch a train. Mostly I just went to poke around. And the more I visited, the more profound my sense of elation. I have no good explanation for this euphoria. A lot has been written about the sense of well-being that we get from well-designed spaces. Christopher Alexander, William H. Whyte, and Tony Hiss are all eloquent on the subject. But the mysteries of Grand Central transcend those theories, sensible though they are. I'm talking about something more irrational, the sense of largesse that permeates everything at Grand Central, the generous spirit that erects a concourse big enough for an aircraft hangar where a room a quarter the size would do. This is the special genius of the place, and what pleases me most.

A few years ago, I moved to the New York suburbs and took a job in the city. Very quickly, I figured out that nearly everyone within a fifty-mile radius felt just the way I did. New Yorkers of my acquaintance talk about Grand Central with a reflexive possessiveness, and never mind that they have no reason to go there for months or years on end (long-distance trains stopped running out of the terminal more than a decade ago; now it just serves commuter trains to the New York and Connecticut suburbs). Like the Statue of Liberty or the Empire State Building, the terminal is one of those places the locals only visit when they have out-of-town guests. Still, the place is an indelible part of what it means to be a New

Yorker. Commuters may be even worse about the possessiveness, but at least we have an excuse. We use the station twice a day. We have something like squatters' rights. I'll bet there are a lot of riders out there like me, for whom the twice-daily transit through the terminal is the highlight of the day.

Now that the $196 million, nine-year restoration of the terminal is well under way, we are determined that "our" station not be monkeyed with too much. Most of the time, of course, we're just too happy for words. As directed by Beyer Blinder Belle, the architecture firm that oversaw the restorations of Ellis Island's main building and the New York Botanical Garden's greenhouse, the makeover is first-class work. As soon as the big east waiting room off Forty-second Street was re-done in 1992, you knew things were going to turn out all right. The waiting room is like the terminal in miniature. The marble floor, the plaster, the fixtures—almost everything that would need work elsewhere in the terminal—would be worked on there first. And sure enough, that stunning overture set the tone. Drop cloths have gone up and down around the building like magicians' capes, and every time they're whisked away, the oohs and ahhs get louder. Parts of the project are massive, such as building a new staircase on the east side of the main concourse, an idea that was included in the building's original plans but never carried out. But a lot of the restoration amounts to clearing away dirt and other obstructions that have dimmed the terminal's original brilliance. We can be happy that the New York Central Railroad was a lazy landlord. The company didn't always keep things in good repair, but neither did it change them much.

Of course the one thing that everyone cared about most— the only thing a lot of people cared about—was the barrel-vaulted ceiling, with its painting of the constellations. People have been crowding into the terminal to see this starry sky since midnight, February 2, 1913, when the doors first opened to some three thousand rubberneckers. Sure enough, the ceiling sparked the project's only real fight. The surface that you see is only about fifty years old. It replaced the original plaster fresco, and some argue that the second version, painted on boards that have been nailed right over the original, is much inferior to it. Others say that's nonsense, and besides, not enough of the original remains even to restore. The younger ceiling's partisans made a persuasive case, and if there was any doubt, it was eradicated when the test patch was cleaned off in the ceiling's southeast corner last year. Who knew that when you washed off a half century of soot and tobacco smoke, you would be able to see all the way to heaven?

I'm only surprised that there weren't more fights, and I almost wish there had been. We need more of the sort of vigilance that sends people to war over a ceiling. Grand Central, so big and so durable, looks indestructible and has for almost a century. But that look has not worked in its favor. When ridership peaked after World War II (64,719,574 passengers in 1946), beautiful space was closed up to make more offices but, *Hey! the place is still handsome, right?* Sure it was. And it was in the fifties and sixties, when ridership fell off and the terminal's owners closed up more space, this time junking up the concourse itself with billboards and big clocks and Kodak's mammoth picture displays. Even then, you could tell it was a great building. You couldn't hurt it. Unfortunately, it took a wrecking ball at Penn Station, across town, to put a stop to that kind of nonsense. Grand Central lives, I sometimes suspect, only because another station died. And even Grand Central's protective landmark status was a battle that lasted through two decades and went all the way to the Supreme Court.

Maybe all the fighting is good—what a New York thing to say. Grand Central was born amid fighting, the brainchild of two architectural firms with very different approaches. From Warren & Wetmore, we got the brilliant Beaux Arts style. From Reed & Stem, who worked closely with William Wilgus, the visionary chief engineer of the New York Central Railroad, we got the pedestrian ramps in the station, the encircling drives outside for automotive traffic, the two-tiered entry system for trains that separated suburban from long-distance traffic, the electrification of the rail lines, and the burial of track and the sale to developers of air rights over that underground track. (In case you were wondering, Park Avenue buildings north of the station have no basements.) Somehow, members of the two firms managed to collaborate, and the result was the greatest building that any of them would ever design. It is as practical as it is lovely, seamlessly integrating a major transportation system into the middle of commercial Manhattan.

So much for the textbook goodness of the place. But wouldn't you rather know that in the information booth there's a hidden spiral staircase that goes down to the information booth on the lower concourse? That hiding off the Graybar Building passageway there's a little movie theater? That if you take the elevator off the ramp to the Oyster Bar and go up one floor, you'll find the Campbell apartment, a room nearly sixty feet long and twenty feet tall, which has a giant fireplace and faux travertine walls and once held a pipe organ, a piano, and tapestries from thirteenth-century Florence?

This is trivia, of course, but the sort of trivia that perfectly matches the greatness of Grand Central, because even the greatness is a little kooky. This was a building that once symbolized the majesty of a railroad. Now we just celebrate the building because it is a transcendent building, art for art's sake almost, gracing each of us who passes through it with some of its spirit. In the 1950s, trying to generate support for the building, *Architectural Forum* wrote an open letter to the city of New York in which the editors called the main concourse "the best big room in America." I keep saying that over and over, I like the sound so much. I'm also sure it's true. It's not the biggest room or the best room, but the best big room. How strange, how unstuffy, how perfect. Grand Central is so grand that we have to make up categories just to describe it.

1997

The Other Upstate

FREDERICK BUSCH

Where we live in Upstate New York, two hundred miles north of Manhattan, is a countryside of wild ridges and hardpan yards, steep, hard worked, and inelegant. It is a land of historic names, as well: James Fenimore Cooper's Leatherstocking country lies over a range of blunt hills, and his Cooperstown is just thirty-seven miles away. This is chewed-out, used-up dairy pasture for the most part, and the farmers, their numbers annually diminishing, work hard and try to hang on. Because of our elevation—close to 2,200 feet above sea level, which we boast of as a farmer might speak of a good yield to which he contributed the work that made the difference—my wife, Judy, and I feel a little closer to the stars. We've seen the aurora borealis stretched up and ashimmer over our horizon, and we get wonderful summer displays of shooting stars. We feel nearer, somehow, to what's wonderful, to what makes us wonder out loud. That is why we stay.

Our countryside is also close to the *Upstate* terrain of Edmund Wilson's memoir and far from that of the Adirondacks. This is what inhabitants of New York's Southern Tier (shaped by Corning and Elmira, Ithaca and Binghamton) regard as northern country. We are considered to be in the uppermost reach of the Appalachian (i.e., signally deprived) region, and our children's large central school received generous grants from the federal government because of it. We are far from the gentility of Putnam, Columbia, and Dutchess Counties, those outposts north of New York City where weekenders in L. L. Bean outfits spend hours refurbishing farmhouses. But though our landscape has its share of small houses seemingly held together by asbestos siding and trailers (some vinyl-covered and double-wide, some rusted-out and small), it also boasts beautiful limestone dormitories, at Hamilton College and Colgate University (where I teach), and high, broad brick churches, like the Baptist church in Hamilton.

Our road is called the Turnpike Road, which connects the village of Sherburne (five miles from us, where we buy our New York papers, if and when they arrive) with New Berlin, about ten miles away (you say "New *Ber*lin," according to local legend, because during World War II the village's name would otherwise have been unpatriotic). We live in an old farmhouse that was once the center of 400-odd acres; 130 of them still surround us, providing the silence and privacy we like, neither of which seems to grow more abundant the longer you live anyplace. The house, at its core, is early nineteenth century: kitchen, pantry, bedroom, bath. The rest of it grew as old houses do, with structures—a living room with bedrooms above it, a bathroom, a guest room—added on. Sometimes the additions first involve subtraction. Opening the walls and ceilings that hid what we were sure would be beams and posts, we found two-by-fours that we removed and replaced, horizontally and vertically, with hand-adzed timbers from a collapsed barn. It was less an aesthetic than a structural matter: The rooms above were bellying down toward the living room.

In the 1980s, Judy dreamed frequently that she rounded the

corner of our kitchen, looked through the dining area, and discovered another room. So she designed it, and our friend Claude Sherwood built it. (Claude has also worked on our house's plumbing and wiring.) We feel a long distance from the kitchen when we sit in there these days, watching storms beat up the valley and over the raised beds of the vegetable garden sleeping under snow. Ours is an ordinary farmhouse, the kind the region abounds in: low, tough, and rooted in against the weather. The people in our area tend to be like their houses. If you want someone to wave to you from the cab of his pickup truck, you might be disappointed. He'll have seen you, though. And if you're stuck in a storm, he'll come and get you out.

There are variations to these country houses, including the high Victorians of rich farmers—usually chafed and worn, needing a roof, too expensive to heat or keep up—and the gloriously clean-lined brick-and-wood houses in nearby Norwich, for example, where wealthy merchants once held sway at the edge of town. One of the smallest cities in New York State, it grew rich on drugs, thanks to Norwich Pharmaceuticals, which eventually became part of Procter & Gamble. It was always a medical town because of Chenango Memorial Hospital, and the grand old houses were well kempt when the doctors, pharmacy executives, and research scientists were in their ascendancy. But Norwich Pharmaceuticals fell upon rough times. The hospital, too, had bad days as well as good, its patients opting for hospitals in Hamilton, Binghamton, or Cooperstown. And the scuffed look of the countryside has infiltrated the little city's borders, which are tinged with a bit of seediness.

Connecting Norwich and our wild ridge, Route 12 passes Pleasant Valley Road. If you look at maps printed before

World War II, you will find it labeled Negro Hollow Road. Drive up its rutted surface, slowly, passing on your left what was once one-room Schoolhouse No. 5 (now a family home), then passing on your right the site of a famous nineteenth-century murder—a man shot and killed his neighbor for permitting his chickens to scratch on the murderer's lawn (we are a prickly lot)—then you will come to a small house, on the north side of the road, the windows of which look like those of a church. Indeed, it once was a Methodist church, with a white pastor and a congregation composed mostly of African-Americans who fled north on the Underground Railroad. Most of their descendants were killed by the Spanish influenza epidemic of 1918. Claude Sherwood remembers a summer job he worked for the town of Sherburne, scything the grass in what was known as the Negro graveyard. Claude was trimming between the stones when it was decided by the town that renovation of Pleasant Valley Road required stones; they were harvested from the gravestones of those Underground Railroad passengers and their descendants. It is a long way for the white folks to have declined, from the moral courage of those who aided blacks on the Underground Railroad to the—let's call it—pragmatism of that roads project.

The surrounding countryside is rough. A fine 150-year-old farmhouse on our road has fallen in upon itself, though people still live inside. Before the house was buried in refuse and by despair, you could notice the stone well house on which dark stones spelling DON'T TREAD ON ME warned interlopers (and modern-day federalists) away. The house itself is now hidden by a derelict camper, and the man who built the well house is gone, as are the Ku Klux Klan gatherings he sponsored on his adjoining field.

But a love of history and good structure still inspires many of the people who inhabit this countryside. On Route 80, you can pass a traditional nineteenth-century coaching inn that is slowly being brought back from wear and neglect by its owners, local furniture makers who acquired it a few years ago. It has a handsome shape (reminding us of our own place) and gives off the sense of regained strength that old houses in good hands can radiate.

Pat and Jeff Kramer, another local couple, have made a Victorian paradise for themselves on a parcel of land abutting state forests. You think yourself in the mid-nineteenth century inside their kitchen or looking at the big house from the bank of their enormous pond. The house is comfortable as well as large, its detailing pure Victorian: curlicues, knobs, shadowy spaces. The interior work, like the more modern work in the room in my barn where I write this, is the product of the imagination of Bruce Webster, a local builder and an artist with wood. Bruce has made a practice of restating the traditional sense of design that made the big farmhouses so tenaciously a part of the acreage they were built on; his structures are spacious, full of privacy—places in which you could dream an interior, as well as administer an exterior life.

I feel the pull of local history, too. In *Sometimes I Live in the Country,* I wrote a novel in which Negro Hollow and its church and the sad end of its inhabitants played a part. Our sons grew up here, and, according to Judy, I almost did. I keep trying to. I have written a couple of dozen stories, at least, and four novels set in this countryside. And I have been called upon to answer for my intrusion into this land of Cemetery Road and New *Ber*lin; a church discussion group took me to task for allowing some of my city-born characters to cast aspersions on mobile-home life, and my explanation—that it was a *character* who spoke, not I—wouldn't wash. A number of copy editors have complained—have despaired—that I angled roads differently from their positions on the map, that I too freely transplanted road names I loved, Bill Potter Road, say, which is not far from us, or Sheridan Hill Road, or the steep, wandering Bear Pass that connects Route 20 with Munnsville. I remind my interrogators that I am dealing with *fiction,* where you make up what becomes the truth. But they want to know how come the road on which Bill Potter once lived cannot remain the road on which he actually did once live. It's a fair question, I suppose, if you're talking about maps, though I am in the business of reconstructing the maps so that we can live on them inside the characters and not inside ourselves.

Certain realities instruct me as my fiction cannot: A well pump eighty-five feet deep is struck by lightning, and the house goes dry; a storm takes down the main branch of a dooryard maple that's a hundred years old, and I am faced with removing all that thick weight from within six feet of our door; three raccoons climb down the spruce in our side yard, their eyes unblinking as they descend upon the nighttime yard, and I mutter about traps and about .22 long-rifle ammunition but simply stand in place to watch them come; coyotes howl over the hill across the road from us, and they do sound like lost, sorrowing souls. And I still wave from the cab of my own old pickup truck more than I am waved to. But, one way or another, that will also become a part of my record of life—as it is lived on roads I'll rename and relocate—in my own version of Upstate.

1999

The Glory of
McKinney, Texas

KATE LEHRER

THIS IS HOW I DO IT: I RENT A CAR AT DALLAS/FORT WORTH
Airport, make my way anxiously north on the crowded
Metroplex highway, and scowl at the countryside defaced by
urban sprawl. After I pass through Lewisville, the half-ugly
view of dilapidated farms and random strip malls never fails
to evoke melancholy. Soon, though, these vistas turn into
gentle rises of rich black farmland, and with a radio station
playing old rhythm and blues and my hand cradling a Dr
Pepper, my spirits begin to lift. I bore into the north Texas
prairie, where I grew up, as did my mother before me.

The heat comforts, the flat land soothes, and the Texas sunlight at its brightest pleases. Those of us native to this sceni-
cally challenged region—beset recently by droughts, floods,
and clouds of grasshoppers—learn to be grateful for small
variations of landscape and to call them beautiful.

Spying the water tower, I begin the gathering up of my
past, collecting scraps of memories, chasing shades of old
emotions. McKinney is thirty miles north of Dallas, and despite a twenty-year spurt in its population from 16,000 to
54,000, old McKinney remains intact. I am home again.

My destination is Courthouse Square, repository of so

many memories of growing up, and its center, the old Collin County Courthouse, within which once lay our recorded hopes and failures—births, deaths, marriages, divorces, crimes, bankruptcies. A courthouse represents community pride and a pioneer boast: We came; we prevailed; we built. Settlers and their followers built and rebuilt this structure with, I suppose, grandeur in mind. As a child, anyway, I considered it grand.

By 1979, however, a new courthouse, built several blocks southeast of the square, had usurped the old one. Collin County wanted to be free of having to maintain and insure the building and offered to sell it to the town for next to nothing. The building languished, nobody seeming to care much. Even the spit-and-whittle club stopped convening on its lawn. Recognizing that unless it refurbished the centerpiece the downtown square would lose its energy, McKinney passed a sales tax to restore the courthouse. Architexas, a firm that had successfully restored a more imposing courthouse in the Texas Hill Country, drew up renovation plans.

All seemed well until the relatives began fighting over the inheritance. A controversy brewed between history purists, who wished the structure to remain unchanged, possibly to be used as a museum, and those who wanted a center for the arts, which would require alteration. Although best intentions informed the argument, a stalemate resulted. Only half in jest, a banker proposed tearing the old courthouse down and replacing it with a parking lot.

Perhaps the quarrel is not surprising, for the building has always reflected change in the culture of the square and the community. After a fire destroyed the first modest, circa-1850s wooden courthouse, its successor, completed in 1876, flaunted a gaudy French Second Empire configuration. For a time it stood as the tallest Texas edifice north of San Antonio. With the coming of the railroad and prosperity, an extensive re-building program began in 1927. The old towers and mansard roof came down to make way for a much-changed centerpiece with a flat roof in the era's fashionable neoclassical style. Ugly yellow-tan brick covered the building's old limestone exterior. When I was in high school, we called the 1927 architecture post-office modern, but it remained McKinney's prime glory, hence the struggle now over how best to reuse it.

Why all the fuss? Sure, the imperative to renew and restore matters to me—and to those who, like me, want tangible reassurance of their memories. But a hundred years from now, what will that courthouse tell anyone? And do our individual memories count for anything much at all? Who will again experience the thrill of stepping into its dim interior? Lulled by the cool darkness and churchlike solemnity, a child could be a princess in her palace or simply a little girl in an imposing space that represented for her the thrill of going to town. A child's imagination can inhabit public places and the worlds they represent.

Having lost much from those worlds, I try, on occasion, to recover some small part.

ON A LANGUOROUS Texas summer afternoon, heat rebounding from the streets and sidewalks, my cousins and I wait, impatient for the end of the nap time instituted by our mothers in an attempt to prevent polio. Our sandals freshly polished, my pinafore starched, we walk six blocks to town with one or another of our mothers, the scent of honeysuckle somehow mitigating the unrelenting sun.

In the courthouse, we weigh ourselves on the tall metal

scale in the lobby and claim our fortune card, the fortune of more interest than the weight. If my mother and I are alone, we will stop two doors east of the square proper at Julia's Hat Shop. Julia lets me try on any hat I can reach while she and my mother, charter members of McKinney's Business and Professional Women's Club, catch up on news or recall their days as star high school basketball teammates. As I listen not so much to their words as to the cadence of their voices and the pleasure in their laughter, my contentment is complete.

Farther down the street is the building that once housed the Ford auto dealership where my mother, just out of high school, kept the books. Although my grandfather apparently had no intention of letting his six daughters either work or marry, he found himself no match for my mother's will or the dealer's respect for her. Never one for domestic life, she went back into the workplace with enthusiasm a year after my father's death at the end of World War II.

That suited me fine, my aunts being more indulgent. Soon my treks to town included more movies at the Ritz, spiffy then and now in its Art Deco facade. A restaurant-and-shop complex today, in its earlier life it was the town's only theater with first-run movies. As we feasted on musical extravaganzas, melodramas, and westerns, we thought Dallas had nothing on us. Nestled beside the movie house, and as much of a treat, was a pencil-thin bookstore. Along with books, it carried a children's magazine—I forget the name, but it printed short stories, the inspiration for my first creative writing.

In a few more years, I would work after school across the square at Martin's Music Store. On slow Saturday nights, Mr. Martin would take out his saxophone when Sy, a salesman in a men's clothing store, strolled over on his dinner hour to take a turn on the drums. Listening to them playing jazz and telling me stories about traveling with swing bands, I could not imagine a more glamorous life, despite their protests to the contrary. Even now on a walk down that street, I hear them and sometimes believe I detect a whiff of the nutty cotton-gin smell heralding fall, new hopes, a new school year.

THE DOWNTOWN AREA includes blocks of stores enclosing the courthouse. Craig Melde, chief architect of the courthouse project, says that it is one of the finest, most intact commercial squares in the state. With styles ranging from late Victorian to Art Deco to modern commercial tacky, the scale of the one- and two-story buildings, most with brick fronts and many with their original cast-iron thresholds, makes them work together and yet reflect the changing nature and dreams of McKinney's inhabitants.

Although most of the usual downtown businesses have shifted westward to the strip malls, now restaurants and antiques dealers thrive in their place. McKinneyites and day trekkers can enjoy the old opera house, now transformed into a restaurant and antiques store. (In my youth it was a Woolworth's, but long ago it was a real opera house, in the tradition of small railroad towns.) Across the square, there's the old Central National Bank building, where my mother deposited her first paycheck, as I did mine. Now filled with antiques stalls, the building, a paean to the notion of temples of commerce, still retains its impressive columns and tiled floors, yet even it can't dwarf the 1927 courthouse or the history that took place on its grounds.

Of course, the courthouse also held darker currents. Helen Hall, McKinney's premier historian, told me about the public hanging there of a man accused of murdering his brother-in-

law; he had protested his innocence to the end. During the
Civil War, nearly thirty saloons dotted the square, which
made the town a congenial place for a bunch of murderous
thugs called Quantrill's Raiders, sent there by the Confederate
government to suppress pro-federal sentiments.

After the Civil War, some of Quantrill's men settled in the
vicinity, according to Jay Crum, a friend steeped in McKinney
lore, and became a reason for Frank and Jesse James to make
frequent visits. In the same pattern, Belle Starr got her mar-
riage license at the courthouse and soon began her life as an
outlaw. Later, in the early 1930s, Bonnie and Clyde made occasional appearances. A young soda jerk who later became
my uncle once served them root beer floats at Smith's Drugs.

Decades after the outlaw era, my friend Gail's grandmother
warned us twelve-year-olds of treachery and danger if we
ventured into town. By the 1950s, crime seemed as remote as
forests and mountains, and we found her predictions hilari-
ous; but undercurrents of a more insidious kind continued to
prevail.

In the luxury of my innocence, I never noticed that a water
fountain was marked NEGROES ONLY and that there were no rest-
room facilities for African Americans at all. I was not aware
that they didn't shop on the square, either. Nor, for that matter, did many Hispanics (we called them Mexicans), except
on Saturday nights during the fall harvest, when migrant
workers came from the Rio Grande Valley or Mexico. I am
told these patterns of limited trade still prevail. Roughly, mi-
norities and the less affluent live on the far east side of town,
while the more affluent, better-educated newcomers, a number of whom have little to do with downtown, have built on
the far west of the city center.

Newcomers who moved into McKinney's older houses

have often chosen to ally themselves with those who wish to re-create a sense of shared history. It is a tribute to these relatively recent arrivals that many have made as significant an emotional investment in the town's past as we few thousand who have memories of other eras. They have infused new energy and new money. More streets are paved, neglected Victorian houses have been restored, and a big community college finally exists. The square teems as it hasn't in years. (For as long as I can remember, its merchants have sought to enliven the area, since McKinney residents have customarily taken their shopping dollars to Dallas and, more recently, its suburbs.) It is not yet on a par with earlier times, when it served on Saturday nights as a stage for townspeople to see and gossip about each other.

As I grew up, the square offered delights in the form of high school football pep rallies, bonfires, snake dances, banana splits, and sightings of Audie Murphy, the most decorated hero of World War II and a Collin County boy. Now it was Gail's father who told us to stay away from Smith's Drugs to avoid the boys standing on the corner. Misbehavior was not a problem, however, since the merchants knew everyone's parents.

We did not know then that we had Collin McKinney—for whom both the city and the county were named (because of his role in bringing settlers from Tennessee and Arkansas to north Texas)—to thank for first making the square such an important part of our sense of community. He sponsored a bill in the early days of Texas statehood to place a courthouse in the center of each thirty-mile-square county so that citizens could travel there and back in one day. He, in turn, could thank the Spanish for this grid system, adopted by them in the 1500s to foster successful communities. The state's county form of government—judge, mayor, sheriff—comes from Mexico's rule of the territory. Six flags over Texas stands for a lot more than the nearby theme park, though Texans do sometimes think the state came straight from the head of Zeus.

DURING MY WRITING of this piece, the factions have resolved the courthouse issue. Public use is the new theme—county and nonprofit groups will occupy the offices, except for the main courtroom. That amphitheater-style room will function primarily as a justice-of-the-peace court, but it will also be used for weddings, performances, and conferences. The balcony overlooking the court is to be restored, and except when the room is used for other events, the original bench and jury box will be placed in the earlier configuration. (Defendants must have found this unusual arrangement daunting, since they faced the jury directly.) A skylight will be reinstated and the walls and ceiling returned to their original dimensions.

What will probably go missing is that sense of familiarity the old courthouse instilled in its occupants, the way employees on a warm day yelled "Hi, there" out their open windows to friends passing by. Or laughed about the latest spit-and-whittle member to go for a ride with the one female who had joined their ranks. That close-knit culture thrives best with open windows and open doors, helping bring the outside and inside together, to circulate more freely.

Maybe those working to restore the courthouse were looking for this: clues to those past generations of Texans and their effect on the culture to this day, not the oversimplified, larger-than-life one but the one that generated fierce, at times intemperate, independence, along with a belief in hard work, generous hospitality, and an innate, if not always acted upon, sense of fairness.

Whether our roots are old or new, many of us desire to build on the history of a place for ourselves and our children—a potent way to touch another time, another people, a part of ourselves.

2002

How a House
Restored a Family

JAMES CONAWAY

THERE WAS STILL SNOW ON THE GROUND WHEN WE SAW IT,
a Greek Revival with the towering frame probity that New
England farmhouses assume in winter, white as the element
in which it sat, going on for too long: hallway, parlor, dining
room, kitchen, toolroom, shed, all strung together in a pyro-
maniac's fond clapboard dream.

The original windows, with the original panes, reflected a
gently undulating sky; trash saplings leaped from the foundation, bracketing the walls. Someone had stolen the granite
stoop. The kitchen floor had fallen in. My wife, Penny, and I
crept down to the cellar unaccompanied by the real-estate
agent, who had already viewed this rock-bottom listing,
shown as a last resort to relatively impecunious outlanders.
She knew all about the stream flowing out of the fen in the
side yard and through one cellar window. Down there, my
foot went through the ice; I was wet to midcalf and still going
when I withdrew, but my attention was held by the rotted,
bowed central beam, fully two feet square and still bearing
adze marks, that ran the length of the house. It had come
from the heart of a tree the likes of which could no longer be
found in the woods.

Five bedrooms upstairs and an aggregate of eighteen empty Boone's Farm apple wine bottles. Platform beds held up with birch logs and strewn with straw. Chairs without arms, piles of clothes like skin shed by another species: hippies, according to local legend, dozens of them, since gone off to Big Sur or Katmandu, following the death—another rumor—of a child born somewhere in the house. Those hirsute denizens of the sixties had communed even in the attic, in cubicles partitioned by birch boughs, where we discovered a very real Puritan vision in the midst of Aquarian squalor: a wooden loom that must have once hummed in the light of a pre-industrial sun.

The house was an incremental disaster, everyone admitted, the sort that could take a young couple under. Cheap is an inadequate belittlement of the price, but the cost of saving the place was potentially ruinous. I had made some money, however, in a fit of literary slumming, and here was a chance for penance in physical labor and some commensurate recklessness. We bought it.

WE DIDN'T KNOW yet that houses can perform functions in our lives that have nothing to do with shelter, investment, or any of the other reasons we give for acquiring them. I was reminded of this truth recently, when we bought another house in the country, not in Massachusetts but in Virginia's Blue Ridge. Although more than twenty years had passed, the thirst for a place apart returned with the force of that earlier experience, and with it came, paradoxically, a feeling of freedom. Freedom to entertain a mortgage, yes, and the problems peculiar to rusticating, but also the freedom to do with this discovery what we wanted and, by implication, to do with ourselves what we might.

The Greek Revival in Massachusetts was located on the edge of what is called the Hill Country, prelude to the Berkshires; our part of it approached de facto Appalachia. The Middle Branch of the Westfield River slid past, daunting with runoff, vaulted by an iron bridge that made Penny catch her breath. She was expecting our third child, and the idea of a toddler gazing down, down into that chasm pushed us both toward dire, watery dreams.

The missing panes let in spring rain, followed by the entomological bazaar that is a defrosting New England. Itinerant carpenters emerged from a winter of unemployment to undertake the seemingly impossible for wages eminently acceptable. One trucked mud from basement to woods, set steel lolly columns under new beams, cross-braced the gently subsiding barn, and installed a raw new floor in the kitchen. Another dynamited the granite shelf on which the house sat so a drain could be laid to divert the stream.

We moved in for the long summer; window glazing became a definition of eternity. We all slept—our son, Brennan, was nine, our daughter, Jessica, five—in the living room, on iron-frame beds from the local dump. By day there were potential pyres of countercultural detritus, dumped with glee from any handy door or open window: bits of furniture, a veritable birch forest, holey blankets, tattered shawls, shirts and pants all flailing on the breeze, doused with gasoline that gasped when the match was tossed in an orgasmic release from the clutter of the past.

There were the small epiphanies: an old harness, a brass hook gone green with age, sea-blue bottles that once held medicine or ginger beer, a penciled message from another century on a rafter in the attic: *Fifty bushels wheat, fifty-two bushels corn.*

. . .

WE AWOKE EVERY morning to the sight of cobwebs in a corner of the ceiling that each morning we vowed to clean away. We cooked on a Coleman pump stove and took our meals on a long plank table (more bounty dragged in from the shed), bathed in the river in the afternoons, and walked up the big hill to the graveyard. In the evenings we read in the brief glow of shared lamps—there was no television, and no reception had there been one—novels, books of what was then called new journalism, children's mainstays. Brennan took on the Hardy boys, and Jess began the long westward migration through Laura Ingalls Wilder.

On warm nights we lay awake for a little while listening to the river, and sometimes to porcupines chewing on the shed wall. Our fatigue derived from the breadth of the task and our knowledge that it was infinite, and awesome. To stop working was to leave undone a job on which another always depended, but the order of things revealed itself in tasks to which the hand instinctively turned.

Taking down walls, we discovered that the lath had all been made from single boards split with a hand ax and put up as splayed renditions of whole boards. They formed intricate woody puzzles, knotholes intact, miraculously revealed as the old plaster came down.

The walls we did not demolish were graced with paper that covered an infinity of blemishes, our predecessors' and our own. Penny, determined to create some unsullied space, papered the guest bedroom above the kitchen with lovely blue primroses on an angled ceiling, around half-windows overlooking what was once the south meadow. This activity preceded the hanging of Sheetrock, which preceded the sanding of the pine floorboards—some eighteen inches

wide—that had originally been cut with a drop saw raised
and lowered by water power; the boards' rough undersides
were dark and gnarly with age.

The envisioned end of our labors was so remote as to be
fantastical; meanwhile, life meant coffee in thick white mugs,
breakfast from a waffle iron heated on the wood cookstove,
raspberries from the roadside. Fly-fishing for trout as wily and
uncooperative as old hounds, and driving the green, green
hills in search of nothing more substantial than another view
of the gentle tectonic discord that had created so many valleys like our own.

"There are people in the woods," a friend in western Massachusetts had told us, and indeed there were. The young
couple across the road, Steve and Vicki, were restoring an old
inn with a concentration of energy and knowledge that made
our labor seem amateurish. We had supper together and became friends, although we envied them their restoration talents and their tools—they even had a special iron for
removing paint from old woodwork—and they envied us our
willingness to be distracted by swimming, fishing, company.

Up the road, the Tuckers invited us to forage in their vegetable garden until we could get one going. The McGinn family constituted a kind of outreach program to the Conaways,
providing baby-sitters, drywall hangers, furniture consultants,
and occasional partiers. Late one August the youngest, Mike,
came down and sat in a corner of the living room and read an
entire summer's worth of *Newsweek* just to catch up on the outside world, while plaster dust—and those cobwebs—drifted
about him in the moderated fury of the ongoing project.

WITHIN THE HIERARCHICAL resurrection of a house lie civilizing acts of improvisation, from rigging a catwalk to putting a

new roof on the barn, to digging a trench under the foundation to let out water from yet another spring. The former job taught me the value of knowing precisely where my feet were at all times, a good life lesson, as they say today. Up there, on the edge of the world, I encountered a red king snake cruising for mice and maybe for swallow eggs in the rafters; I don't know which of us was more surprised.

Five feet under the earth, I found an intricate, silted-up drain of flat stones laid long ago for the same purpose that brought me there and a preserved log that had been hollowed out lengthwise so water could pass beneath the old wagon lane.

I say civilizing because such economies teach patience and foment an ingenuity uniquely suited to the objective, a waning commodity in the national psyche; such acts link present and past in a way that circumvents technology and provides unblinkered glimpses of lives unseen and remedies lost.

Oddly, the images that endure from our own life are not those of the finished job or the accomplished effect but of the process: I can still see Penny standing in the branch of Sears, Roebuck in the run-down metropolis nearest us, holding paint cans and rollers, her hair up in a scarf and a bit of bare, childbearing stomach showing behind her bib overalls. She is the picture of the beautiful, bountiful American pioneer, but on the face of the sales clerk is an expression of disdain, for he is no doubt thinking, More hippies.

I see Susanna as a baby on the grass, unhappy with her corral; a few years later she is stretched out buck naked in the hammock, a plum in her mouth and on her head an old tin pot. I see a bottle of champagne sticking out of a snow bank one New Year's Day, where I left it after the midnight revelry with friends from a neighboring town. I see Jess sitting on the edge of the porch, eating cake frosting out of the pot that was once on her sister's head; I hear Susanna ask her, "Do you like this bug house?"

I see Brennan and a boy from out of valley attacking me with runty apples, a cardboard box my body armor, an empty plastic spackling bucket my helmet. Their glee resides in assaulting an authority figure with impunity and in the echoes of their expert marksmanship; the dog has fled. Gone now too are those stunted trees that endured all my children's clambering before succumbing at last to the Hill Country's amazing storms.

WE NEVER SPENT a whole winter in our Greek Revival and in the end moved farther away from it rather than into it, as we had once fancied doing. I had a job and so, after many summers of freedom, succumbed to a number of the other sort; the house was now a burden, or so we decided, and after the usual difficulties involved in marketing country property, we sold it, loom and cookstove intact, to a pair of childless schoolteachers from Baltimore.

The result was not the feeling of relief we had expected but the kind of regret that descends in a final moment of lucidity. In my case it came the day before closing, in the cellar where I had spent untold hours with a shovel. The two-foot-square beam was long gone, the spring a moist, enduring reality. This was the 1980s, when grown men cried only over real estate that had not tripled in value, and ours hadn't quite done that. But I wept for a lost aspect of our lives that had been in the intensity of our common endeavor, I now saw, extraordinary, and irreplaceable.

If we had not bought the house, it would have collapsed. That knowledge helped. But the real significance, I think,

resided in the structure that had revived us even as we restored it, at a time when we didn't know exactly what was
missing in our lives, only that something large and difficult
was required, something more than career and domesticity.
We had in a sense started over with this house, pushed
through tangible problems as well as some personal ones,
and if we had not solved them all, well, we had at least set
aside the bigger ones until, when finally looking down, like
searching for tools long left in the grass, we found them altered or altogether gone.

Driving over the iron bridge that day, gazing back at the
big white facade, I remember thinking with absolute certainty
that two schoolteachers from Baltimore could not handle
such a place. The house needed and would always have us.
Only this delusion made the break tolerable; only the acquisition of another house twenty years later makes writing
about that one possible now. In a year or two we would buy
it back, I thought at the time. Meanwhile, they had our telephone number; they would no doubt be asking regularly for
advice about the cellar drain or the wiring in the attic, calls
that never came.

1998

The Water Under
the Bridge

PAUL MARIANI

A STEAMY JULY AFTERNOON IN LOWER MANHATTAN three or four years ago, the temperature near the 100 mark. All morning I have walked about Greenwich Village and the Lower East Side, looking for signs of Hart Crane's having passed this way, trying to get into the poet's mind by glimpsing the buildings and landscapes—however altered—he would have known here eighty years ago. And given that this is New York, a city that eats its past the way sows eat their own young, I know it is not going to be easy uncovering that world. Here and there traces of cobblestone pavement, the streets and alleys following the haphazard planning of the city's colonial forebears, the mid-nineteenth-century brownstones and Georgian structures that Poe, Melville, and Whitman walked among. One imagines Crane in this or that structure: some two-story brick-fronted building with a central hall, already converted into apartments back in 1920, the poet playing his striated records of Ravel or Richard Strauss on his wind-up Victrola, typing on his portable late into the night, moths circling the electric bulb above his head, the ghostly words giving him solace, blessing him with their heady delight:

Through the bound cable strands, the arching path
Upward, veering with light, the flight of strings,—
Taut miles of shuttling moonlight syncopate
The whispered rush, telepathy of wires . . .

It is the Brooklyn Bridge, one sees, that Crane kept coming
back to, finally locating an apartment at 110 Columbia
Heights, on the Brooklyn side of the river that flows beneath
it. The building is gone now, torn down after World War II,
the space part of the Watchtower complex. I know portions
of this river, have known them since anything I can remember, though my part of this flowing, this curriculum in a pur-
ple twilight, lies farther uptown: at Astoria, or just above the
Queensboro Bridge, or, a bit later, down at Fifty-first Street.
Now, on this sweltering July day, walking across the Brooklyn Bridge as untold millions have done, and with Hart
Crane's long 1930 poem, *The Bridge,* haunting my mind, I am
seeing the river again, this time from a great height. And not,
at least this once, am I seeing it from a car. That I have done,
of course, any number of times these past fifty years, in a
hurry to get from one destination to another. No, this time I
take in the view almost like a tourist or, better, a recording
angel. There below lie the vast sweep of the river, the rotting
piers, the eternal seagulls whirling and dipping below, the
low-rise tenements and the trees, maples and sycamores, as
in Crane's day, and—above me—the massive cathedral-like
Gothic pilings supporting the untold miles of bound steel cables.

There is so much history here; for this is the Roeblings'
dream, first the father's and then the son's. Boss Tweed and
Tammany Hall, Walt Whitman's vista in "Crossing Brooklyn
Ferry," Governor Al Smith's boyhood haunts, City Hall, the

South Side piers, the Woolworth Building—that "nickel-and-dime tower" paid for and built by the department-store mogul, the city's tallest skyscraper for nearly two decades, until the Empire State Building went up in 1931, rising incredibly in spite of the worst depression the country had seen. Hart Crane's white buildings gleaming in the light of a summer day. An impossible dream so beautiful, so charged with erotic vitality, it hurts, as it hurt García Lorca when he was here in the late twenties, and hurt Scott Fitzgerald's Jay Gatsby, and William Carlos Williams, looking at this same city from the vantage of that other great river, the Hudson, as he dreamt of its tall buildings and women from the cemetery rise in Rutherford, New Jersey.

Hart Crane wrote in 1924 that he wanted to be remembered, always, as looking at the great Manhattan skyline from the window overlooking the East River from his rented rooms at 110 Columbia Heights. In all seasons he stared out on the impossible city gleaming before him, Odysseus bewitched by his Circe. "Everytime one looks at the harbor and the NY skyline across the river it is quite different," he told his mother that May,

and the range of atmospheric effects is endless. But at twilight on a foggy evening . . . it is beyond description. Gradually the lights in the enormously tall buildings begin to flicker through the mist. There was a great cloud enveloping the top of the Woolworth tower, while below, in the river, were streaming reflections of myriad lights, continually being crossed by the twinkling mast and deck lights of little tugs scudding along, freight rafts, and occasional liners starting outward. Look far to your left toward Staten Island and there is the Statue of Liberty, with that remarkable lamp of hers that makes her seen for miles. And up at the right Brooklyn Bridge, the most superb piece of construction in the modern world, I'm sure, with strings of light crossing it like glowing worms as the L's and surface cars pass each other going and coming.

How extraordinary, he summed up, "to feel the greatest city in the world from enough distance," from some vantage where one could at last see it in something like its full splendor and vitality. Too often, walking its streets, lost among its canyons, with the blare of taxis and trolleys behind him, or the clack of the elevated cars overhead, one was simply "too distracted to realize its better and more imposing aspects."

STANDING THERE, ALONG the escarpment overlooking the East River on this July afternoon, I suddenly understood Hart Crane's New York, his lost Atlantis, his benzine-rinsed white buildings rising majestically across the wide waters of the river. I have studied with wonder the grainy black-and-white images of this river preserved on damaged celluloid from the 1920s: ghost tugboats wheezing up the river past steamships bound for Buenos Aires, Liverpool, and Calais; sailing ships moored in the harbor along the wharves on South Street; the Gothic pilings of the Brooklyn Bridge slowly rising; or— downriver—Lady Liberty with her colossal torch welcoming immigrants to the new world, my own grandparents from Italy, Poland, and Sweden somewhere among them.

But this sight—this river and this city seen from this vantage—even with Hart Crane's windows at 110 Columbia Heights long vanished, along with Crane himself: This struck with the force of a revelation. People passed me, deep in thought or conversation, or just walking their dogs, while I

stared and stared. In the mind's eye I see it still and will probably go on seeing it for the rest of my life: a river, a force, the
Woolworth Building and Wall Street directly ahead or slightly
to the left. And up to the right, the cathedral of the Brooklyn
Bridge sleeping in the afternoon sun, its enormous force for
the moment placated, at rest.

CONSIDER FOR A moment the lenses of Picasso, Juan Gris,
Braque. The river as Cubist mélange, from seven or eight
vantage points.

CHRISTMAS NIGHT, 1995. Returning with my family from
Greenwich Village, the station wagon loaded with gifts, up
around Seventieth Street on the FDR, heading north and
stuck implacably in the glue of traffic. Movement by inches,
if at all, and tempers flaring. On the other side of the steel di-
vider, headlights zooming south. Ahead of us a river of tail-
lights flashing dully, then brighter, as cars came to a full stop.
Twenty minutes, half an hour, four or five city streets tra-
versed, swearing under my breath. Everyone growing tense.
Then the phosphor-red police flares, and cops directing us to
the left. Then the sight of the ambulances lined up on the ex-
treme right, and three cars badly smashed, their passengers
about to be rushed to the huge hospital opposite us on our
left. Here then, in the anonymity of the great city, a life, or
several lives perhaps, ended. Just then I caught myself looking out beyond the ambulances to catch a massive tug churning through the darkness of the river. *Le Néant,* the Abyss.

SUMMER, 1947. I am seven years old and have come down to
the river. There is a park here at the eastern end of Fifty-first
Street, where my mother has often brought my brother and

me to play. But today I have wandered down here alone, crossing the FDR, to walk out on some of the ancient rocks facing the river. Somewhere near here Nathan Hale, a Connecticut schoolteacher and spy for General Washington, rowed ashore on a reconnaissance mission, was intercepted by British troops and hanged. History. That world, like colonial New York, long gone. Like nature, this city abhors a vacuum. If it can be built upon, New York will build on it. Only here, and out in the river, as William Carlos Williams noted, recovering from an operation in the same hospital near where the accident would happen, is there any sign of the original Manhattan island: three small rock outcroppings, too small for building on, and left now only for the gulls to soil. I stand at the edge of the water here and look out, desiring to embrace this river. Only a man in a topcoat, standing alone and off to the left at the highest point of the low outcrop, intrudes on the scene. Weirdly—if anything that happens in New York can truly be said to be weird—I find the man addressing me. I watch him as he pulls something from inside his coat. A derringer, he says, as he points it at a low-flying seagull.

DRIVING DOWN FROM Massachusetts, where I now live, I often take the FDR into the Village or to midtown. And there is the river, off to my left, the railroad bridge, the islands with their buildings, a few trees, the Fifty-ninth Street Bridge, which for years was my landmark. Cobblestoned Sixty-first, between First and Second Avenues, where my father was born in an Italian enclave, mostly people from Milan, Turin, and the hill towns east of Genoa. Here too in the late 1930s my young mother came, fresh from Paterson, New Jersey, with her widowed mother, a good-natured, hard-drinking Swedish flapper, whose dead husband, fresh from Poland, had joined Black Jack Pershing's army in Texas and rode a horse named Red across the Mexican border in hot pursuit of the elusive Pancho Villa. That was the year, 1916, that a boy named Hart Crane decided to make his name in New York, two miles downriver from the spot where my father was born. Forces melding in the imagination, married yet isolated, like those islands gleaming in the river.

1948. MY STEP-GRANDFATHER, Hank Cosgrove, married to my Swedish grandmother, walks his daughter, my brother, and me along the walkway edging the river somewhere around Seventieth. A bracing breeze comes in off the water. The sun beats bright as a bell off the wave caps in chiaroscuro fifths. Hank has a package of animal crackers in his pocket, from which he has been carefully doling out treats. He points to an island out in the river and to some derelict buildings there. His father, he says, died on that island, fighting a fire. They went into the building and the flames trapped them, he says, and the men died there. His father, a big New York Irishman, was one of them. He was a hero, Hank says into the air, to no one in particular. Can I have a cookie? I say.

Great flakes of wet snow falling on the river, the whitecaps roiling, coursing southward to merge with the great Atlantic, far from the Christmas lights of Macy's and Bloomingdale's. The gray gulls sullen, withdrawn and unblinking, perched on the tops of the rotting piers, themselves slowly going under, to merge, as everything will, with the river.

THE WILLIAMSTOWN THEATRE, midsummer, three years ago. My wife and I have driven up to this college town in the northwest corner of Massachusetts to see a play called *Dead*

End. The setting is New York City in the 1930s. It's a drama rife with issues of social justice, the American Depression. The set is a piece of New York in remarkable detail: brick-and-marble-fronted buildings along the river at Fifty-third, tenements and a posh hotel side by side, representing the stark economic contrasts endemic to New York. The actors are dressed in the film styles of the thirties. Like them, too young to have known that world firsthand, I let my memory roam, checking the accuracy of the set against the black-and-white films and photographs of the period. The acting is good, the accents are believable, but the scene is wholly imagined, for these buildings never existed in this place, right up against the river. Still, it's all somehow right. My mother swam the East River as a girl. A strong swimmer, she dared the whirlpools up near the Hell Gate Bridge, aptly named. I recall boys swimming in the polluted river, in a film I saw as a boy myself back in the 1940s. The film was called *The Naked City*. Real boys swimming in black trunks or in their underwear. A fictive murder and fictive cops, fictive lines recited above a celluloid river. The river remembered, the river imagined. And the real river, like God, flowing outward forever. Yesterday, today, and tomorrow. *Per omnia saecula saeculorum.*

IN THE SPRING of 1932, Hart Crane was returning from Mexico City with a woman, the ex-wife of an old friend, a woman he imagined might become his wife. It was the nadir of the Depression. Crane's millionaire father had died the year before, broken by that same Depression, leaving his son virtually nothing. Hart was returning to New York and the East River by ship and was 275 miles north of Havana when he did what he had been daring to do for years and killed himself, leaping from the ship's stern and disappearing beneath the waves. The body was never recovered. Fifteen years later, his mother's ashes would be scattered from the midsection of the Brooklyn Bridge, that metaphysical span in a physical world, a bridge reimagined by the poet himself. From here his mother's ashes might descend, like black snow, to merge with the river below. Perhaps in time in this way she would be reunited with her only child, from whom she had been es-tranged in his last years. A belle in New York once, dancing the latest steps, the Charleston among them. Now she too, like her Hart, has made the great leap.

THE TRAFFIC THIS winter day along the FDR, heading in either direction, as well as along all the approaches to the river, has been backed up for nearly an hour. Once again everything has come to a standstill. The bright morning sun reflects off a thousand car windows and seems to be laughing. The eighteen-wheel rigs and the buses, too, are sitting idly, diesel fumes misting the air. It's New York on any given day, really. Only the river, with its ghostly clippers and steamers, its spent history renewing itself as the eye moves along its whitecaps, seems to be moving inexorably onward.

2000

Song of Sonoma

STANLEY ABERCROMBIE

F OR MORE THAN THIRTY YEARS, THE IDEAL CITY, FOR ME, meant only and precisely New York. An escapee from a small textile-mill town in west Georgia, I had arrived eager for everything the big city offered. "The rumble of the subway train, the rattle of the taxis" were music to my ears, at least for a very long time. After three decades, the rumble and rattle began to lose some of their charm, there began to be a few unpleasant incidents in my city existence (my lunch snatched off my plate at one of Manhattan's few outdoor cafés, perhaps explaining why there *are* so few, and a memorably large knife pointed at my stomach in a broad-daylight stickup), and I began to wonder if such incidents might be less likely elsewhere.

Of more importance was age. I suppose thirty years anywhere will make you thirty years older, but I know from experience that thirty years in New York will. There comes a time when, with diminishing energy, one begins to resent spending so much of that energy simply going from the West Side to the East Side, arguing with sullen grocery store checkers, stepping into winter gutters of icy gray slush, and defending one's club sandwich and fries.

So, a few months short of my big Six Oh, attached to New York work commitments only by an invisible stream of electrons, and accompanied by my friend Paul, who was equally enthusiastic about a change, I made a second escape, this time to Sonoma, California (population: 10,000; major industries: a dozen wineries, two cheese factories, a turkey farm, and a few orchards; speed: slow). As I keep telling incredulous old friends back east, I love it. Those old friends, indeed, are the only things about New York I truly miss, and fortunately the California wine country is an area many of them seem willing to visit. As for the rest of the city that I loved so well so long, a week or two a year there is enough to sample some new restaurants, catch some theater, and remind myself why I left.

After almost three years in Sonoma, I still find it delightful. I love the wine, of course; it seems a civilized pleasure driving through vineyards, watching the vines grow, seeing the grapes picked, smelling the crush. The resultant bottle of wine, however, can be drunk anywhere—not just in Sonoma, but even, I must admit, in New York. Some other Sonoma pleasures are more strictly local. I'm proud of the thick-walled 1840 Mission San Francisco Solano, where occasionally, with great acoustics, chamber-music concerts are given. I delight in the oaks spotted on the dry hills, the rainless summers, the potato-rosemary loaf from the Artisan Bakery, the artichoke-topped pizza at the Bear Flag Café, the intricate little Oriental chests at Sloan & Jones antiques, the Fourth of July parade (forget marching in step, just enjoy the costumes), the used books at Chanticleer and the new ones at Readers'.

Most of all, I enjoy my wonderful new freedom from overcoats, scarves, gloves, hats, and occasionally even shoes, and those electrons linking me back to the office never tattle about footwear. I also delight in the absence of things here: Miracle of miracles, fast-food drive-throughs have so far been kept to the edge of town, and downtown shops, though a mixed bag in quality and interest, are all local, independent enterprises rather than franchised repeats of the usual mall components. There is no Wal-Mart, no Gap, no Ann Taylor, not a single Starbucks. Commercial Sonoma, in short, has managed to maintain a quite identifiable personality.

You probably detect a pattern in this roster of delights, but I'd be embarrassed to tell how long it took before I saw the pattern myself, before I realized that my view of Sonoma was simply as a cornucopia of sensual pleasures for me to see, to eat, to drink, before it dawned on me that I was using this town as a visitor might, not as a resident should. Fine as life here continues to be, I hope my relationship to the town has begun to be slightly less hedonistic, slightly less selfish.

I have begun to wonder how this identifiable civic personality has been achieved and who we Sonomans are. Some families have been here for generations, obviously, and others began with weekend retreats from San Francisco, an hour south, then moved here full-time. The important thing is that the majority, like me, seem to have come here for no other reason than wanting to be here, a very good reason indeed and one that leads directly to feelings of contentment, if not smugness. My assessment on arrival here (New York dirty, noisy, dangerous, too cold in winter, too hot in summer; Sonoma clean, quiet, safe, a perfect climate) still seems true, at least for this particular person at this particular stage of life, but, all the same, a great oversimplification. I am beginning— just beginning—to see their town as Sonomans do, which, naturally enough, is not in contrast with the way New York is now but with the way Sonoma was then.

The traffic, for example. Having to circle the historic little Sonoma Plaza twice before finding a parking spot (two-hour limit, free) seems to me no hardship at all, even though traffic is sometimes halted while a hen or a parade of ducks crosses the road, heading to or from the pond just west of City Hall. For the longtime Sonoma resident, though, twice around the plaza is a new and unwelcome nuisance, and never mind that traffic in Manhattan is a thousand times worse.

And crime. Like many small-town newspapers, ours features weekly a half-page of items from the local police blotter, items that by the standards of New York (or Chicago or Detroit or Miami or you-name-it) seem less like crimes than minor discomfitures or the results of naïveté. Learning that you can't leave a toolbox on the seat of an unlocked pickup anymore only leads to astonishment, for us newcomers, that you ever could.

And building restrictions. When, shortly after my arrival, the celebrated San Francisco restaurateur Pat Kuleto announced plans to occupy an empty building near the plaza, I assumed most of the town would share my enthusiasm. The permit for his new restaurant was denied, however, because the on-site parking lot held a few less cars than the Sonoma Planning Commission considered appropriate. Accustomed to restaurants opening without a care in the world for how their patrons might arrive, I found this response quite puzzling. Kuleto dropped his plans, the building is still empty, and I often pass it with a touch of regret for the dinners that might have been.

If I at first had been surprised at some of these local manifestations of self-protection (and, I must admit thinking, overprotection), I am even more surprised at how easily I am coming to accept them. Maybe parking requirements for restaurants make a lot of sense, I'm beginning to think. By the time it takes three and four circuits around the plaza to find a parking space, I will probably be a confirmed Sonoman clucking about the good old two-circuit days.

The sad thing is that the four-circuit days are probably inevitable. Sonoma, I fear, cannot keep its numbers of businesses, people, and cars at the present level. It may lack the will, and it surely lacks the power, to halt its own growth. I worry about the town's will from reading the local paper; for, despite some bold city steps (like the one about Kuleto's parking lot) and despite the admirable activist impulses of some volunteer citizens' groups, many of the letters printed in the paper and many of its editorials advocate a much softer, more laissez-faire attitude. Planning and guidelines are fightin' words for some of our citizens. Even for myself, I hesitate to take the unattractive position of "Now that I'm here, please bolt the door." And I know Sonoma lacks the power, because, after all, every town and every city lacks the power; a complete curb on growth would require measures much more draconian than would ever be found acceptable in a democracy.

If the present size and character of Sonoma could somehow be frozen as they are today, the surrounding towns and cities would continue to grow and the new people there would drive their new cars straight into the heart of old Sonoma. Like in *Jurassic Park,* we can warn them to stay in their cars, but they won't. The more distinctive the town is able to keep itself, the more desirable a destination it will become. The more picturesque, the more popular. The more individual its shops and markets, the greater a magnet they will be for those communities suffering international homogenization.

The problem is not that Sonoma is changing and Manhattan isn't. Jan Morris's *Manhattan '45*, published in 1987, tells the bittersweet story of a city that no longer exists, a city of Hudson River ferries, elevated trains, and trolleys, of Schrafft's and Longchamps, of Harry James playing at the Astor Roof, Billie Holiday singing at the Onyx, Sherman Billingsley welcoming Sophie Tucker to the Stork Club. Since 1945, Manhattan has changed almost totally, and by no means have the changes been all bad.

But we expect Manhattan to change. It lost control of its destiny ages ago, and present efforts at shaping and improving that destiny are fingers in the dike—necessary and desirable, but with limited and unpredictable effectiveness. Sonoma, on the other hand, is not only so obviously worth protecting but also so small, so definable, so relatively understandable that it gives the illusion that protection might be possible. It isn't.

It must have been a decade since I last saw the term *population explosion;* it must have been a couple of decades since that term described a hot topic; and it must have been much longer ago than that when anyone seriously considered doing something about it. Distasteful as population control now seems to many, our population does continue to explode. Although, through the improved status of women and the improved state of contraception, fertility rates are dropping in many parts of the world, the overall picture (according to an article published last June in *The New York Times*) is that the present world population of 6 billion is expected to grow to 11 billion before stabilizing sometime in the twenty-first century. We, in our increasing numbers, are the enemy.

And what will happen to our little town as our numbers increase? As its population grows from 10,000 to 100,000 Sonoma will change from a small town to a small city. Jane

Jacobs pointed out in her landmark 1961 study *The Death and Life of Great American Cities* that cities "are not like towns, only larger. They are not like suburbs, only denser. They differ from towns and suburbs in basic ways, and one of these is that cities are, by definition, full of strangers." As a town grows, therefore, its inhabitants' serendipitous contacts with acquaintances, on sidewalks and in shops, in banks and bakeries and video stores, will increasingly be replaced by contacts with strangers.

We can live with that. One of the things that appealed to me so much about New York when I was young was, in fact, the blessed anonymity that its numbers offered, compared with what seemed to me to be the unbearable nosiness of a small Southern town. But strangers tend to treat us less benignly than acquaintances do. Already, I have begun to realize that all is not as idyllic here as it appears. Sonoma County, I learned at a recent AIDS benefit, has the highest rate of HIV infection of any rural or suburban county in the United States. And in Santa Rosa, the county seat half an hour north of Sonoma, a young man was recently killed in the third gang-related slaying of the year, and the number of gang-related crimes has roughly doubled every year since 1991. GANGS GET A FOOTHOLD IN THE WINE COUNTRY said a recent headline in *The San Francisco Chronicle*. VIOLENCE, CRIME FLARE IN SONOMA COUNTY.

That police-blotter item about the toolbox theft isn't, apparently, the end of the story if the whole county is considered. Even my favorite potato-rosemary loaf and my favorite rainless climate had a tragic convergence last summer, when an uncontrollable fire in the dry grasses burned a couple of thousand acres, forced a number of hasty evacuations, and destroyed the bakery owner's house.

So all is not as perfect in Sonoma as one at first assumes,

or as permanent and safe as one hopes. But we, its citizens, are not helpless bystanders. I have begun to see another thing. In addition to the many earthly pleasures that the town can give those of us who live here, there are a few things we can do for the town—there are organizations that invite our participation, causes that need our support, meetings that deserve our attendance: among others, the Friends of the Sebastiani Theater, the Sonoma Valley Citizens' Advisory Commission, the Sonoma Citizens Coalition.

This last group, recently advertising its first public meeting, published these questions: "How can we control increasing traffic, tourism, commercial and residential development? How can we preserve our historical, ecological, educational, cultural and agricultural heritage?" And these answers: "In tackling these issues, more involvement by Sonoma citizens in the decision-making process of government is essential, if we are to avoid being overwhelmed by increased growth and economic pressure. No longer can you afford to stand on the sidelines."

It's not that I'm contributing anything yet. I'm not still standing on the sidelines—not exactly—but I'm just sitting and listening, and it may be a long time before I stop feeling too much an outsider to speak my mind at these meetings. But they are teaching me that urban problems are relative, that it is not only people who age and change but also cities and even small towns. The Sonoma of the future cannot be the Sonoma of the present, but at least it has a good head start. It has been, as we used to say back in Georgia, well brought up. I'll bet that, given the attention it deserves and the guidelines it needs, it will grow into something that continues to be pretty special.

1997

Grand Entrances

EDITH PEARLMAN

IN 1942, AT THE AGE OF SEVENTY-FIVE, A FRENCH ÉMIGRÉ DIED at his home on East Eighty-sixth Street in Manhattan. *The New York Times* identified him only as a retired architect who had lived in Manhattan for four years. The notice made no mention of the particulars of his work.

Yet Hector Guimard—like Baron Georges Eugène Haussmann, like Gustave Eiffel—left the city of Paris permanently adorned, and New York should have noticed. A century ago Guimard imagined, and then drew, and then constructed, entrances to the new Parisian subway system, called the Métropolitain—*le Métro*. Eighty-six of his entrances still stand, guarding the stairs that plunge into the subway. Along with the Eiffel Tower and the boulevards, they are the emblems of this generous city, where More is More.

A railing surrounds the sides and back of each stairway, made not of clunky stone, not of monotonous spikes, but of medallions shaped like shields, side by side by side, in frames of flowing ironwork. Every medallion incorporates an *M,* sometimes high-shouldered, sometimes squat, its long arms ending in curlicues.

The railing's color is the green of spring. Above it, twin

posts rise. Each unfurls into a kind of flower that is also a kind of eye: an ovoid bulb set in a pair of petals like lids. The station signs, made of powdered limestone, use an idiosyncratically shaped alphabet, including proud heads on the *T*s, *R*s with swooping tails. Railings, posts, signs—all promise an easy descent into the underworld.

Hector Guimard was France's chief practitioner of Art Nouveau architecture: romantic, abandoned, sensuous. Not the stuff, you'd think, that would attract a middle-aged husband and wife returning to Paris for an idle look at the Watteaus in the Louvre and perhaps a single brave ride on the grand Ferris wheel at the place de la Concorde.

But it did attract us. And it inspired us. In fact, it turned us into zealots.

WE WERE ALREADY more or less fans of *le style Métro*. Years earlier, our children had loved it; on late afternoons the sight of green railings and fanciful signs assured them that their cultural forced march was over, at least for that day. Soon they'd be sitting in a subway train reading their Astérix comics.

On this visit without offspring, who have grown and flown, we discovered that Paris is engaged, with self-congratulatory flourishes, in a three-year project to restore and refurbish the familiar entrances. We learned a lot from the accompanying publicity. In 1899, Parisians thought that Guimard's designs were crazy, but *que faire*? The Tour Eiffel had already made them a laughingstock. The designs were executed, and the changeable citizenry grew fond of them, though the Commission of Old Paris fretted about the bizarre alphabet. Then, three years into the work, Guimard was dismissed. Public opinion had determined that the place de l'Opéra, the home

of Jean-Louis-Charles Garnier's opera house—that grande
dame of the hysterical Beaux Arts—would be debased by an
édicule (a little structure) in the Guimard style.

His style fell further out of favor through the years. Art
Nouveau surrendered to Art Deco; exuberance succumbed to
the Depression and war. Some of Guimard's entrances were
slowly destroyed by neglect. Others were uprooted and carried off by foresighted collectors. In 1978, public attitudes
having flip-flopped once again, the entrances were written
into an inventory of historical monuments—a *supplemental*
inventory; no point in being headstrong. And now, more than
two decades later, they were scheduled for reconstructive
surgery.

We resolved to visit them. Not all eighty-six, for we had
only one week and there were those Watteaus to look at. But
a few.

WE VISITED A great many. As collectors know, enthusiasm
grows with acquiring, and every Métro entrance we saw became another acquisition in our collection: similar to the last
but different, too. Each used some, and usually many, motifs
from Hector Guimard's repertoire—crescents and hooks;
stalks and branches; curved struts. They were not repeated
motifs only; they were modules, for Guimard was a man of
his industrial time. He turned all his designs over to the
Foundry of Saint-Dizier for execution, ensuring that the elements would be uniform. Municipal structures are meant to
be recognized, after all. That decision also ensured that the
elements could be freely combined and recombined into
works of art. Guimard chose cast iron for his material because, unlike wrought iron, it lends itself to curves. Nothing
is harsh, nothing pointed.

Sometimes the railings around the stairs form a wide U, sometimes a narrow one. Sometimes the posts are truncated. At Château d'Eau, two entrances face each other on the same sidewalk, suggesting that the stairways will soon cozily connect (they do). The Louvre's Métro entrance, the narrowest possible, has only an L-shaped railing; the museum itself provides the third side. Chardon Lagache is softened by surrounding chestnut trees; but at Blanche, a place relatively treeless, the cast iron is almost the only green in sight. At Mirabeau the paint looks fresh—evidence of restoration. And Monceau offers a framed legend about the restoration project, which intends to honor not only Guimard and not only Art Nouveau but also the materials themselves—lava from Auvergne, limestone from Burgundy.

For the entrance to the Bastille station, Guimard designed and built a large structure resembling a pagoda. But we saw its intended magnificence only in a photograph: The pagoda was dismantled and presented as a gift to New York's Museum of Modern Art in 1958. Two other elaborate structures do still stand, though, at Abbesses and Porte Dauphine. Their projecting roofs are nicknamed dragonflies, and with good reason, for panes of glass soar diagonally upward, forming a transparent wing for the traveler's protection. At Abbesses this dragonfly roof shields the usual cast-iron railing. Nearby, children whirl on a carousel; trees scatter their leaves; nursemaids gossip. The scene is enchantingly Parisian. But at Porte Dauphine the dragonfly's wings hover above not a three-sided railing but a three-sided wall. And what a wall—peach-colored panels made of lava and greenish ones made of glass. This orange-and-green delight is only a Métro entrance, yet it looks as if it might shelter a small dance floor and even a master of ceremonies.

The man who made a subway station look like a cabaret—
what was he able to do with a house?

We dashed into the Louvre to see the Watteaus, and dashed
out again.

Guimard's Parisian buildings, those that did not fall to the
wrecking ball, are in the fashionable northwest corner of the
city. Some were intended as private mansions but are now
apartment houses; others were apartment houses from the
beginning. Constructed of stone and brick (this was before
the heyday of glass and steel), they are nonetheless light on
their feet, with curvaceous asymmetrical facades. Flanked by
stodgy contemporaries, they look like roués among school-
marms.

Guimard gave loving attention to every element of his
work; in the treatment of windows he was a particularly brilliant haberdasher. In the building at 142 avenue Versailles, for
instance, the ground-floor windows are topped with plain lintels proper to the small shops that occupy this area. Then the
windows get dressed up; on the first floor they wear a delicate carved halo, on the second a pointed Gothic hood, on
the third iron caps. From the mansard roof, four windows
look out from deep cowls, like curious monks.

On the house Guimard built for himself and his bride at
122 avenue Mozart, a balcony wraps ardently around the corner of the building. Black ironwork enacts an enchanting
writhe. The hewn stone surrounding the entrance has been
carved into flowers—or are they waves, or are they Madame
Guimard's curls? He signed this work of love with his mono-
gram, in his own witty alphabet, incised into stone.

The Castel Béranger at 14 rue la Fontaine was built as a
medium-rent apartment building. It soon became home to
artists and interior decorators and delighted eccentrics. The

grilled gate, all curves and swoops, looks like a cello married to a harp. Sea horses climb the wall. Balconies wear iron faces that resemble Japanese masks. And all this cast-iron trimming is the very green of the Métro. Stained glass fills doorways and windows—stained glass in pale colors, its panes cut into Art Nouveau arabesques.

Guimard was said to have been a difficult man, and at the end of his life, forgotten and far from home, he must have been a disappointed one. But in his prime he behaved like a hot-blooded suitor, bestowing on Paris airy domiciles in which even the homeliest necessities—vents, coal chutes, drainpipes—were extravagantly decorated, and creating for her pleasure and convenience delicate Métro entrances, one after the other after the other.

For a little while the fickle city returned his love; then she sent him packing.

WE RUSHED TO revisit Castel Béranger on our last day in town, after what had become our usual noontime spin on the Ferris wheel. A window on the ground floor had been flung open in order to air an apartment being painted. By climbing onto a ledge we could peer inside, see the curved moldings and the plaster flowers that seem to grow from the wall, see also the workman with the brush in his hand. He saw us too; open-mouthed, he stared at the pair of untidy gray heads that had popped up in his window.

"Look! Hector's carvings," we cried. "Look! Hector's swirls."

"Oui," soothed the painter, not wishing to derange us further.

2002

An Anthology in
Clapboard

JAY PARINI

F OR EACH OF THE PAST FOUR SUMMERS, MY FAMILY AND I
have spent a couple of weeks living in a nineteenth-century
farmhouse that once belonged to Robert Frost: a white clapboard dwelling with a small screened-in porch and a steeply
pitched roof designed to shed the heavy winter snows. The
Homer Noble Farm is hidden from the road, as if still protecting the privacy of its most famous owner, who lived there
quietly each summer from 1939 until his death in 1963. The
150-acre farm, which skirts Middlebury College's Bread Loaf
campus in Ripton, Vermont, is owned by the college and
maintained as a memorial to one of America's greatest poets.

I often teach a seminar on Frost at Middlebury, and this
past fall term I took my students to the farm, hoping that
some of the atmosphere would rub off. Before the class arrived, I planted a boom box with a tape of Frost reading
"Mending Wall" behind the Victorian couch in the living
room, with its sloping wide-plank floors and stone fireplace.
We sat around for a couple of hours talking about the poet as
afternoon shadows lengthened and the room grew dusky, almost dark. I purposefully did not turn on any lights. At the
right moment, I said, "You know, the house is haunted by

Frost. In fact, if you listen close, you can almost hear Frost himself talking." While the class tried to take in their professor's burst of madness, I pressed a button on my remote device and Frost's gravelly voice was summoned from the shade: *"Something there is that doesn't love a wall / That sends the frozen-ground-swell under it, / And spills the upper boulders in the sun."*

I don't think those lines have ever made a stronger impression on a group of students.

I've been writing a biography of Frost for several years, so my stays at the farm have been useful. The house is still redolent of the poet, as if he has just passed through the living room into the kitchen to make a cup of tea. Some of the furniture and many of the books on the shelves are his. Indeed, I found a thirty-year-old note to Frost between the pages of a forlorn book of poems in one bookcase. It could have been written by me. "Dear Mr. Frost," it read. "I have admired your poems over the years. I wanted you to have this volume of my own poems—a meager tribute to your own great gift."

I have always loved the poetry of Frost for its simple eloquence, its sturdy colloquial rhythms and rural imagery, and for the idea of poetry as "a momentary stay against confusion." It would be only a slight exaggeration to say I was drawn to Vermont, where I have spent most of my adult life, by Frost. In high school in northeastern Pennsylvania, I memorized many of his poems, including "The Road Not Taken," "Stopping by Woods on a Snowy Evening," and "Mowing." When I was fourteen, I visited Vermont with my parents on a summer vacation. I told myself then I would live in Frost country one day. And I do.

The Homer Noble Farm (every Vermont farmhouse is known by its previous owner) might easily be a film set for the poems. The deep pastures that surround it are the sort that Silas in "The Death of the Hired Man" would come home to hay. A small orchard beyond the west field would make a perfect setting for "After Apple-Picking." The dry-stone wall separating this farm from the next would seem to confirm the famous line from "Mending Wall": "Good fences make good neighbors." From the upper pasture, one sees range after range of mountains, "one behind the other / Under the sunset far into Vermont," as the poet wrote in " 'Out, Out—.' " To the north, a stand of paper birches seems just right for the boy in "Birches," who spent his free time climbing those snow-white trees until his weight bent them back to earth.

On the northern slope behind the farm lies a thick woods, where I often walk with my children. One day, a couple of miles along a leafy path, I came upon a tumbledown house with a hemlock growing right through what used to be the country parlor. This might well have been the place Frost had in mind when he wrote "Directive" in 1945. That magnificent poem begins:

> Back out of all this now too much for us,
> Back in a time made simple by the loss
> Of detail, burned, dissolved, and broken off
> Like graveyard marble sculpture in the weather,
> There is a house that is no more a house
> Upon a farm that is no more a farm
> And in a town that is no more a town.

Behind the house, I found "a few old pecker-fretted apple trees" much like the ones Frost describes. I also found an overgrown wagon road over which would have traveled "a buggy load of grain" to the barn, which is now a skeleton of light.

. . .

FROST MADE THE Homer Noble Farm his base of operations from late April through early October. From the 1920s, he had been associated with the nearby Bread Loaf Writers' Conference. There, he lectured on poetry and read his poems to adoring audiences every summer for nearly four decades. As one Bread Loafer from the 1930s recalled: "The whole point of coming to the conference was to see Frost in action. He was the living embodiment of the American poetic tradition, and he knew it. But it wasn't arrogance. Whatever respect he got was earned. His voice—even when he spoke casually— was weighty, although he was often joking. He was the spirit of the place."

The first Vermont farm that Frost owned was in South Shaftsbury, near Bennington. But in 1938, after the death of Elinor, his wife of forty-three years, he began to cast about for a new place to live. The old farm had too many memories, and they tore him apart.

The director of Bread Loaf in 1938 was Theodore Morrison, a Harvard professor and novelist. He and his wife, Kay, were close friends of the poet, and Kay had recently become Frost's secretary. The summer of 1938, just after Elinor's death in the late spring, was a strange and wild time for Frost, who was forced to cope with immense grief, loneliness, and un- certainty. He was, as he said, "rescued" by the Morrisons, who became in effect his new family.

The Morrisons had been renting the Homer Noble Farm from the widowed Mrs. Noble, who now lived in the village with her daughter. Frost was smitten by the place, and a rumor that it might be for sale excited him. Throughout his life, he had had a keen eye for property; he had bought and sold several farms in rural New England over the previous five decades. He went directly to Mrs. Noble and made her an offer that she could not refuse. (By now, Frost had plenty of money—his most recent book of poems, *A Further Range,* had been a huge bestseller, and he was regularly paid handsome sums for readings at colleges around the country.)

One feature of the farm that attracted him was a small log cabin on the north side of the house, which remains to this day a kind of shrine for poets and admirers of Frost. It was built in 1928 by Mrs. Noble's adopted son, Harold Whittemore, who rented it to hunters in the fall and fishermen in the spring. The cabin boasts a massive stone fireplace in the living room, pine paneling on the walls, one bedroom, and a kitchen large enough for one grown man to stand in and boil an egg. One of its best features is a shaded screened-in porch, with a view of mountains rising in the middle distance. It backs up against a vast forest.

Frost immediately saw the possibilities of the place: He would sleep and write in the cabin while Ted and Kay Morrison would occupy the main house, which is separated from it by a five-minute walk through a maple grove. A ring-down intercom connected the two dwellings, so Kay could call and say that dinner was ready. The Morrisons, who loved the farmhouse and liked the connection to Frost, were only too willing to comply with his fantasy. Kay would come up after breakfast to help Frost with his correspondence—he was endlessly fielding invitations to read his poems at colleges far and wide. She would carry back to the main house any manuscripts or letters that needed typing.

Lunch and dinner were taken in the main house at a rustic maple table just off the kitchen. There were often guests— faculty members from Bread Loaf, young writers wishing to pay homage, local friends. Frost's several grandchildren were also frequent visitors. Among those who lived nearby was

Rabbi Victor Reichert, whose summer house was only a few miles from the Homer Noble Farm. "We started coming here in the early forties," remembers Louise Reichert, the late rabbi's wife. "One of the great attractions, of course, was Robert Frost himself. My husband and he would sit up late discussing philosophy and literature. They became extremely close friends."

Staying up late was a habit with Frost, an owl by nature. "He was also one of the best conversationalists who ever lived," says Peter Stanlis, a Bread Loaf student in the 1940s who became another lifelong friend of the poet. "Students would go to the cabin after dinner, and Frost would talk. His conversation ranged widely, from politics to metaphysics. Of course, he loved to talk about poetry, too. He had read everything. And he talked in this slow, resonant voice, lingering over a phrase, purposefully repeating himself, saying the same thing a different way. The hours would slip by. Midnight would come and go. Frost would stay up all night if you were willing to listen."

Frost liked to walk in the woods, to "go botanizing," as he put it. "I once walked with him in the woods behind the cabin," recalled Reginald L. Cook, who taught at Middlebury College for several decades. "Frost suddenly stopped by a tree that had a strange mold growing around the trunk. He wouldn't rest till we had gone into town to the college library to find a book of molds. He wanted to know the precise name of this particular mold." Indeed, the *Collected Poems of Robert Frost* offers a remarkably thorough guide to the flora and fauna of Vermont and New Hampshire.

Having been a farmer in Derry, New Hampshire, at the turn of the century, Frost never lost touch with the soil. Although he farmed only intermittently after 1913, he preferred to live in a place where agriculture was happening. He enjoyed dipping his hands in the earth and was never without a garden. At the Homer Noble Farm, he opened a plot of ground in a field just to the east of the farmhouse, planting beans, lettuce, tomatoes, and peas. Even in his late eighties, he would spend a certain amount of time each day with a hoe in his hands or bending over his plants. The garden offered not only a means of getting some exercise but also an endless storehouse of metaphors—his poems glisten with them.

The main farmhouse feels rooted in time past. A potbellied stove in the kitchen recalls a different era, when microwave ovens and automatic can openers did not exist. A stillness seems to gather in this house, clinging to the old furniture and books. There is no hurry here: The hush of the house seems to militate against it. In the early mornings, I often linger on the stone porch after breakfast, letting the sun warm my face as bees swarm around a nearby thistle. I watch a garden snake bake itself on a slab of rock. A bluejay flutters from branch to branch in a tall white pine.

One of the odd pleasures of this house is an old claw-footed tub in the bathroom. I fill it to the brim in late morning, then soak there for half an hour, reading. I like to imagine Frost in this tub, his feet poking through the water, the sun streaming in. He often stayed in the main farmhouse when Kay and Ted weren't there, and he would certainly have used this tub. He was, his neighbors always claimed, a "lazy farmer," one who slept in late, took long baths, puttered about the garden as if there were all the time in the world.

An old friend of the poet once told me a story I will never forget. He was driving Frost back to the Homer Noble Farm after a dinner in nearby Bristol. It was a moonlit August night, with huge stars in the sky. The driver mused, "On a night like this, I keep thinking that life is so short and there is so little time." Frost put a hand on his arm and said, "It's the other way around, you know. There is so much time. More than anyone could ever need."

LIKE MOST OLD farmhouses in New England, the Frost place has small windows—a defense against the withering cold. This makes the house a bit dark, except when the sun is streaming through those windows directly. At the north and east ends, huge pine trees overshadow the house, adding to the sense of darkness in the main parlor. On most days, even a slight breeze creates a strange, whooshing sound. Frost was fascinated by this natural phenomenon and in a poem called "The Sound of Trees" wrote about it memorably:

> I wonder about the trees.
> Why do we wish to bear
> Forever the noise of these
> More than another noise
> So close to our dwelling place?
> We suffer them by the day
> Till we lose all measure of pace,
> And fixity in our joys,
> And acquire a listening air.
> They are that that talks of going
> But never gets away;
> And that talks no less for knowing,
> As it grows wiser and older,
> That now it means to stay.
> My feet tug at the floor
> And my head sways to my shoulder
> Sometimes when I watch trees sway,

From the window or the door.
I shall set forth for somewhere,
I shall make the reckless choice
Some day when they are in voice
And tossing so as to scare
The white clouds over them on.
I shall have less to say,
But I shall be gone.

Frost managed to get the sway of those trees into the rhythm of the poem. He understood the allure of this wailing, almost unnatural sound that is, paradoxically, the essential voice of nature itself: the groan of invisible wind caught in the high branches. The idea that we "suffer" the trees is perversely wonderful: They (who are going nowhere) tempt us to go away. Like the Sirens who lured sailors to their death in ancient Greek myth, the trees—or the sound of trees, more precisely—draw the listener into a zone of danger.

One day last August, I sat outside the Frost house with a volume of his poetry open on my lap, my back against a pine tree. Suddenly the wind overhead began to whine and moan; the big pine started pitching, "tossing so as to scare / The white clouds over them on." I felt like running away myself. "The Sound of Trees," the poem and the phenomenon itself, seemed vividly real to me.

FREUD ONCE SAID that houses symbolize a dreamer's soul, and his observation seems especially true of writers. More so than most, writers occupy their houses completely; they live and write there, often over many decades. The house grows into a physical manifestation of the writer's spirit as text and architecture intermingle in odd, affecting ways. This is certainly the case with the Homer Noble Farm. It is a living anthology of Frost imagery, a place apart, a repository of Frostian emotions. The poet is strangely, even frighteningly, present here—an alluring figure who beckons from the nearby field, saying, as in "The Pasture," "I sha'n't be gone long. —You come too."

1998

Hamlet in the Hills

DAVID HUDDLE

"Won't nothing bring you down like your hometown."
    —songwriter Steve Earle

WHEN PEOPLE USED TO ASK ME WHERE I'M FROM, I'D often say southwestern Virginia. Or the Blue Ridge Mountains of Virginia. Or what we now call Appalachia. Or Wythe County, down Interstate 81 about halfway between Roanoke and Bristol. Or I'd say that I went to high school in Wytheville. Or that my house was about nine miles from the intersection of Interstates 81 and 77. Or even that I grew up just a few miles from the Appalachian Trail. I was never comfortable saying the actual name of the place. But nowadays, ask me where I'm from, and I'll say it right out loud—*Ivanhoe*. In a crowd of people at a cocktail party, I'll answer a little louder than necessary, *I'm from Ivanhoe, Virginia.*

Maybe I've grown up enough to stop being publicly ashamed of where I come from, but I'm still divided about the place—and still writing about it. Each time I updated my backup file for this essay, my computer asked me, "Do you want to replace the existing Ivanhoe?" Of course, I never failed to click on YES. That's how it's always been with me. Because it makes me uncomfortable, I try to replace the real Ivanhoe, in every story and poem I write about it, with some other place, some other topography. In my fiction, I've even renamed it Rosemary. But no matter what I write, the "existing Ivanhoe" remains, in my mind as well as on the map.

When I say it, I see it—*Ivanhoe,* the way that little cleft in the hills holds about as many houses as you can hold Monopoly buildings in the palms of your two hands. The two-lane highway sends you along a winding ridge, so that at certain points your eyes can take in almost the whole hamlet. There's a higgledy-piggledy logic to how the dwellings align themselves along the three sides of the valley, the narrow road snaking down beside the Ivanhoe Branch (in Vermont, where I now live and teach, we would call this the Ivanhoe Brook) toward the center. Church Hill, across the way, shows you how the land has resisted settlement. Like many of the houses, the Forrest United Methodist Church, the Pentecostal Holiness Church, and the Church of God of Prophesy all have a high wall and a low wall to accommodate the steepness of the hill.

In the evolution of this community, nothing has been officially planned—no one house looks like another, and every building site has its own slanted configuration. One church is made of cinder block, another of white clapboard—with red mud stains along its foundations—and another is set decorously back in a grove of trees. The houses range from a tumbledown sprawl of connected outbuildings to the tidiest of white ranch houses with carefully tended flower beds along the front walkway. But even within the chaos there's a barely discernible pattern, something hidden and unexpected. If the lay of this land produced some tilted thinking, it also forced a grudging cooperation among the rough customers who settled in here.

Ivanhoe is still not incorporated. There's no government, which means that as long as the deputy sheriff isn't around, you can do anything you want. My own great-grandfather was shot and killed right in the middle of town. A grade school classmate of mine was sentenced to life in prison for slitting a man's throat with a butcher knife. Even the word *town* seems inaccurate for Ivanhoe. People don't behave like that in *towns*. If it hadn't been for the civilizing influence of the three churches and the Ladies' Aid Society, the place would have been designated a war zone. When I lived there, from my birth in 1942 until I went away to college in 1960, distrust of outsiders was first on Ivanhoe's list of community values. If you were a stranger—meaning that you were from farther away than about ten miles—you'd have been out of your mind to take an after-dark stroll down past Price's Store, where the men gathered to sit and talk.

In 1988, friends of mine—academics, a married couple with their daughter—were on their way back home to Vermont from a sabbatical year in Palo Alto, California. They were taking the southern route and driving north from New Orleans up through the Carolinas. On the map they saw they'd be passing within ten miles or so of this place that I'd written so much about in my poetry and fiction. They thought they'd give it a look and then come back and tell me that they'd seen the town and that it didn't look all that tough. They even thought they might drive up to my mother's house, introduce themselves, and chat awhile. As it turned out, when my friends approached the center of Ivanhoe in their Honda Civic bearing a Vermont license plate, they received such hostile glares from the formidable characters they passed that they didn't even roll down the windows to ask directions. Later on, when they gave me their account of the adventure, they made it clear that Ivanhoe was a lot more frightening than my writing had made it out to be.

The neediness of the people seemed to have seeped into the dirt and rocks. The Ivanhoe of my childhood was one of the most marginalized pieces of landscape I've ever known. When I was growing up, the county eliminated the local high school and began busing the Ivanhoe kids each day to and from the consolidated school in Wytheville, fifteen miles away. Just as I reached adulthood, the New York corporation that controlled Ivanhoe's only real source of income, the National Carbide Company, closed down the plant, leaving some two hundred men without employment. At a certain point, poverty gets mean and ugly. There's a look and a smell to a house where people have lived without money for many years. Old clothes and toys and car and machine parts are discarded and let lie to rot and rust wherever they fall. Pass by here and you'll suddenly understand the origin of the phrase *turn your nose up;* it's not just your nose, it's your whole face that responds to a house so beggared that it stinks.

But in spite of Ivanhoe's history of poverty, violence, hostility, and ignorance, its citizens have always possessed a pride that baffles anyone who encounters it. If you live in one of those decrepit houses, you don't stay indoors, hiding and groveling in your shame. You come out onto your falling-down, cluttered-up porch to cuss at the people who walk by, turn up their noses, and then pretend not even to have seen your house at all. You come out to the fence and call them names.

In the old days, that combination of being simultaneously

disadvantaged and prideful put a chip on most of our shoulders and made a few of us downright dangerous. Knives were the weapon of choice for Ivanhoe's bad boys—one of them pulled a switchblade on me once and thus enabled me to discover speed and agility I hadn't realized I possessed. Chaperoning a dance for high school kids, my father took a drawn pocketknife away from another one of those boys. Fire, too, was a weapon or an instrument of entertainment. The Ivanhoe school building was burned down twice, and in 1989, Price's Store burned to the ground.

In more recent times, a grassroots organization, the Ivanhoe Civic League, has arisen under the leadership of a charismatic local woman, Maxine Waller. Mostly because of Waller, Ivanhoe has received grant support from such sources as the Virginia Foundation for the Humanities and Public Policy and the Appalachian Community Fund in Knoxville, Tennessee. It has also gained enough national attention to entice college students from all over the country to volunteer to spend their spring break working to improve the place and help the people who live there.

Waller and her team have gone a long way toward turning Ivanhoe's pride in a positive direction. Nowadays, strangers—kids from colleges in Massachusetts and Wisconsin and Vermont—are welcomed into town and into homes that they are allowed to clean and paint and repair. Conversations take place between the locals and the faraway outsiders, and the returning students I've talked to say that their week of volunteer work taught them to respect the people they met. Ivanhoe's atmosphere is no longer hostile; the town looks lots better than it did while I was growing up: The trash has been picked up, the houses have been painted, and the old Norfolk & Western Railroad track has been replaced with a nature trail. But the area remains disadvantaged. In spite of the civic league's efforts to attract industry, there's only one place to work, a factory that makes rubber gaskets; for the most part, you have to travel elsewhere to make a living. All Ivanhoe has to compensate for that missing necessity of community life is what it has always had—its baffling pride. Those people don't have a dime to their name, and yet they act as if they've got a Mercedes parked on the other side of the shack. When I try to understand this mentality, I can't help thinking that it has to do with the valley itself, those hills, that red clay, that mountain weather.

As a boy, I spent many an hour in the company of the hired men who worked for my grandfather, a gentleman farmer and the New Jersey Zinc Company's engineer and chemist for the area. His men were kind enough to let me witness their austere lives and therefore understand the privilege of my own. Then for a couple of years I was Ivanhoe's paperboy—the one who delivered *The Roanoke Times* to the eighty or so local subscribers. Every morning, I walked a four-mile circle up and down the hills of the town. My feet still remember the stones of certain pathways and strips of road. More important, I spoke with the people, often just a hello or a good morning, but sometimes we'd have conversations about school or family or weather or what my grandfather was up to "now that he's getting some age on him." From this distance of 45 years and 850 miles, I realize that I was raised in part by all those citizens who talked to me, paid me for the newspaper, and offered me water or iced tea, or invited me into their kitchens to warm up on cold mornings. These were people with little money or education or knowledge of the greater world, and yet they had such a delicacy in their manners—such a careful way of taking me in and finding out about my life while also informing me of theirs. Perhaps that courtesy and gift for genuine connection come from a place where houses and churches have to be built with a high wall and a low wall. Where convention can't bully consciousness, the possibilities open up for both negative and positive behavior. I've rarely witnessed the straightforward viciousness I saw in Ivanhoe, but I've also never felt more courteously received into someone's home.

"Oh, that's a beautiful part of the country!" So often this comment is what I hear when I tell someone where I grew up. The beauty of southwestern Virginia isn't the first thing I think to tell people about, and so I always feel a little bit ashamed that strangers have to remind me of it. Sunlit fields of alfalfa, the bend in the New River up near Bilsby, the path up the mountain to Bill Dalton's house, and the winding road at dusk when we would head over to Hester's Drive-in—all those vistas I've remembered from my childhood are at least as valuable as my college courses or my trips to the Smithsonian or the books I've read or even the household possessions that have passed down through the family to me.

It's funny, but I don't think we ever talked about that beauty. Nobody in my family, none of my friends or acquaintances, no teacher in school, nobody I knew in Ivanhoe ever waxed eloquent about the natural beauty of the place where we lived. It was all around us; we just didn't mention it. Which is not to say that we ignored it. On the contrary, what I hope to be the truth is that we lived that beauty—we took it into ourselves the way we experienced the weather and breathed the air.

A spectacularly antlered deer once presented himself to me and my grandfather and the men who worked for him while we were threshing wheat up in Jim Early's hilltop fields. The deer loped down the hill to within twenty yards of us, leaped a fence, and disappeared into the woods. This was on a sunny day in a spot where, had he been there, Albert Bierstadt might have set up his easel to paint the sweep of what we could see during those moments of sublime beauty. Rolling summer-gold fields made up a foreground. Then, tucked down in the valley, were village houses and churches, beyond which flowed the New River, with the green-blue rise of the mountains in the distance. That summer of the deer, I was eleven years old, grown-up enough to help with the farmwork but still very much a child. What did I do upon seeing the animal? The men and I responded similarly and spontaneously—we whooped! We hollered! The ones who wore caps waved them. My grandfather, who was bald, took off his hat and fanned himself with it, though he was sitting on the shady side of his truck. I know it's a romantic idea, but on this occasion of my trying yet again to "replace the existing Ivanhoe," I'm going to stand on it. Such dignity as we possessed came to us out of the air, the water, the sky, and the dirt—the unmentionable glory—of that place where we lived.

2001

Views from a Bench
Above the Sea

ANTHONY WALTON

I HAD NOT THOUGHT ALL THAT MUCH ABOUT THE SIZE OF TWO Lights State Park in Cape Elizabeth, Maine (I thought it, quite simply, quite sincerely, infinite), until I came upon a description of it in a tourist guide as "a vest-pocket park." This means, I surmise, that its seemingly ample acreage is far more modest when compared with such vast public properties as Baxter State Park, whose forested square miles could consume Connecticut for supper, and have Rhode Island for seconds. Maine is also home to the ever glamorous and oversubscribed Acadia National Park, no slouch in square miles itself and with the added benefit of sitting square by the Atlantic, which makes it seem even larger.

Maybe that's why Two Lights has always felt so big to me: Its forty acres of ring lichens, grass, false heather, sea rocket, beach roses, elderberry shrubs; Scotch, pitch, red, and white pines; junipers, balsam firs, black spruces, cedars, crab apples, and, as far as I can judge, Norway maples; slate, granite, sunlight, and wind jut into the ocean on Cape Elizabeth, five miles or so down the coast from Portland.

Cape Elizabeth—the geological formation, not the preppy-yuppie suburb of that same name—marks the entrance into

Casco Bay, one of the largest deep-water havens on the East Coast, shielding Maine's southern shore from the at times brutal northerly and easterly winds of the North Atlantic. The calm waters of Casco Bay, coupled with Portland's relative proximity to Europe (it's more than a hundred miles closer than any other major U.S. seaport), made Portland, founded in the mid-seventeenth century, a center of international trade at one time.

Two Lights derives its name from the presence of twin lighthouses, which until 1924 deployed a fixed light on the east tower and a flashing one on the west, the only twin lights on that stretch of the coast and a welcome landmark for sailors and fishermen working their way toward Portland and a safe berth.

To reach Two Lights Park, you fork left after driving for a couple of miles down a badly paved road on a narrow finger of land with modestly upscale oceanfront houses on either side. On my first trip there, in October 1989, I was certain I'd gotten the directions wrong; no signs pointed the way to the undeveloped oceanside park. (Maine's attitude toward signs seems to be: If you don't know where you're going, why do you want to be there?) Unable to find a place to turn around, I was seriously worried about how I was going to explain my presence to the police, who, I expected, would materialize on my tail at any moment.

Then I saw a sign with an arrow, so I pressed right at the fork—and, before my eyes, there it was. I came over a rise, and the first thing I could smell was the bracing salt of the breeze off the ocean. I caught a glimpse of the wide blue to my right, cruised past an empty guardhouse—admission to the park is only charged from April until October—and found myself in a large, well-graded gravel parking lot. I quickly parked and ran up a narrow, overgrown dirt footpath, unsure of what I would find—and there *I* was. I like to think I'm not a writer prone to overstatement, but in that moment I knew I had found my true home in the world.

I am not a native of Maine, having moved there in 1989 after experiencing the usual indifference and outright dismissal endured by many a young writer who has set out to make his fortune, without any idea of what that entails, in New York City. This was the New York of Bensonhurst and Howard Beach, of Yusuf Hawkins and Tawana Brawley, and I, a young black man from the Midwest, was finding it all a bit much to take. I knew enough about Maine to realize that I would never really fit in; though the natives were polite and, to use a wonderful old almost-forgotten word, even *cordial,* I was "from away," and a flatlander at that. But I wanted the sober quiet and lingering wildness of the state. There is something to be said for not being in your neighbor's business and for your neighbor not being in yours; and if a Mainer, to this day, invites me into a private home, that's a pretty sure signal of real regard if not friendship. I have found these unspoken but enduring codes better, for me at least, than the ever-shifting allegiances, as I read them, of New York and Los Angeles.

I came to Maine with a book deal for what would become *Mississippi* but without much else in the way of finances or resources, and to be honest, I had no real idea of how I was going to write the manuscript I'd promised to deliver and earn the advance my father was (not without reason) so suspicious of: "You mean they're giving you this money, but it isn't yours; you haven't done anything yet?" Yes, they were, and I was going to spend the next five years traveling my loved and dreaded state of Mississippi—the state both my

parents hailed from—trying to "find out who I was." Two
Lights would figure into that, too—but on that first day I saw
it, the park merely represented my access to another beauti-
ful body of water. Having grown up just outside of Chicago,
I had spent hours driving alongside and vacationing on Lake
Michigan with my family. I have also spent a lot of time on
Florida's Miami Beach, with its clear, clear light; on the lush
Gulf Coast of Mississippi; and in mythic—at least for me—
Malibu and Santa Monica. But in all of this vast and varie-
gated American natural beauty, Two Lights is the place I have
visited most, the place I have come to inhabit. It has become
the strangest and most sacred of all places to me.

It is difficult, perhaps impossible, to say why certain places
more than others "speaketh to our condition," as the Quakers
say. I have seen a rough, disarranged sort of beauty in all the
Maine coastal parks—Popham Beach, Reid, Seawall, Acadia,
and Cobscook, to name several—a beauty that has something
to do with life pushing through catch-as-catch-can, even
thriving, under the worst extremes of wind and salt and cold.
At Two Lights, the most exposed of these parks, the highest
point affords a panoramic view. On your left (as you look
toward the water) spreads the open Atlantic to Casco Bay—
on a clear day, and from the correct angle, you can see
downtown Portland with the naked eye. The view to your
right is endless; I imagine, or like to pretend, that you can see
all the way to Europe, or Africa, or even to the tip of Brazil,
jutting out into the South Atlantic.

When I'm feeling really expansive, or silly, I turn and face
west from that highest point in the park, and imagine in the
topographical map of my mind's eye that I can see the continent unrolling before me—there the Appalachians, the Cum-
berland Gap into Kentucky, on to the Mississippi, find St.

Louis, and roll up the wide Missouri to the Continental Divide. Near that highest point is a bench planted into granite, which I've come to think of as my bench. I've often seen other people in the park, but never in all my visits have I seen anyone sitting there, on that bench, and perhaps this is another reason why Two Lights has seemed so large to me.

Further reason, I think, for the vastness I feel sitting or standing there is that something vast does happen, or, to be more accurate, begins to happen, at that part of the Maine coast: It changes. The coastline from York to Cape Elizabeth is relatively straight and uncomplicated, with few islands; after Cape Elizabeth it assumes the gnarled and craggy rockbound visage most of us picture when we think of Maine. Just miles south, at Crescent or Scarborough or Old Orchard Beaches, the coastline more resembles the gently sloping sand beaches of Cape Cod or Long Island. There are, of course, exceptions, but the feel is distinctly different in points southward, more open, with the landscape much less violent, if that is the word.

At Two Lights, the bedrock of the southwestern Maine coast is clearly visible. As David Kendall writes in *Glaciers and Granite*, his fine book on the geology of Maine, the "rocky cliffs are being torn apart by storm waves, exposing folds and faults in three dimensions." A particular rock formation dominant here, schist, looks very much like stacked driftwood but is anything but. Another Maine geologist, D. W. Caldwell, writes in *Roadside Geology of Maine* that "the numerous folds and faults at Two Lights State Park probably date from the Acadian mountain-building event of Devonian time," which is to say 380 million years ago. The rocks of the Cape Elizabeth formation, stretching from Two Lights to well north of Wiscasset, some fifty miles away, sit inside the Norumbega Fault, a gap separating the Avalon terrane, the coastal region, from the rest of the state. Rocks east of this fault resemble the rocks of Europe more than they do those of North America, leading geologists to believe that the Avalon terrane was once part of Europe during the early Paleozoic age.

All this talk of deep time, however, cannot account for why I feel so safe, so *secure,* at Two Lights. It is the place where I experience *calm,* where I am at peace with myself and the world, the place where everything leaves me, the place where I am, in Emersonian terms, emptied and can become his "transparent eyeball." "I am nothing. I see all." It's where I've come to know, in my bones, that both Emerson and Thoreau were on to something, that nature can not only please and educate but also heal. I sit on my bench, basking in the sun (or nuzzling myself in the drizzle, as the case may be), watching the azure water, so sparkly, so cold. The wind, let's say from the west, is very brisk but not overpowering, just on the edge of being unpleasant but is, instead, invigorating. I'm counting the waves, shallow and foamy on this particular day, some of them rising into a clear green spray that is most soothing to watch.

It's the kind of day, the kind of place, I was looking for when I was writing *Mississippi,* slogging through some of the darkest chapters in American history, reading about the slave trade, the plantation system, lynching, Reconstruction, sharecropping, and all the rest, and being shocked each day by what I read. Two Lights is where I came to let go of all of that, to prepare for another day of hard slogging, and I think that is when I fell in love.

So much in love that I'll come in the middle of January, or on a cold day in March, or in December, as I did on the day that has become my most treasured Two Lights memory. More than a decade ago, we experienced in southern Maine a syzygy, an extremely rare astronomical event in which the earth, sun, and moon line up in such a way as to exert an abnormally strong gravitational pull; as a result, we had the highest tides of a hundred years. On the day of this event, we simultaneously endured a gale-force storm, with 50 MPH winds and icy rains blowing sideways. The water rose over the approaches of the old Million Dollar Bridge in South Portland and over U.S. 1 through the Scarborough Marsh. I went out to Two Lights to appreciate the storm's force, but also as an act of fidelity, as if to a lover; I wouldn't just be there on the sunny days. I was joined by ten or twelve other hardy souls, including a young woman whom I shall ever remember, who sprinted by me in a yellow rain suit, bowed at the waist to stride into the wind and sleet, and looked back at me to grin and yell, *"Isn't this great!!!"* It was.

One more thing: I am aware that my most treasured place sits surrounded, threatened, by another place and a way of life that may yet kill it. North and south and west, new houses have begun encroaching upon the park. There have always been those fortunate enough to live on the Maine seacoast, but now the houses, yuppie palaces, Saab-culture cottages, call them what you will, are being wedged into every possible place and built in every conceivable shape. The state of Maine is experiencing a massive influx of retirees and those who have made their fortunes elsewhere and who are now flocking to the quiet, rugged shores of the state. But their arrival has meant higher property prices, higher taxes, and a not so subtle distortion of the landscape and cultural values they purported to have fallen in love with in the first place. As a result, many locals have been forced to leave.

This disturbing trend epitomizes much of what I think is wrong with American society today: economic segregation (and with it, segregation of race and class), the so-called winners seceding from the rest of us and building their own locale and existing as if the old troubled America, the late social activist Michael Harrington's "other America," didn't exist. Is this what we as Americans have to show for our Roaring Nineties? I can imagine, on my darkest days, a state government administration, under tremendous budgetary pressures (just a decade ago, Maine faced deficits in the hundreds of millions), auctioning off a "vest-pocket park" to the highest bidder. With such pressures in today's economy and real estate market, is it too much to speculate that the park might someday not be there to enjoy?

Stunned to drive the perimeter of the park and see all the houses, I look at a street map of Cape Elizabeth—once a quaint little burg of rock-ribbed Republican rectitude; I used to joke to my friends that if Barbara Bush were a town, she would have been the old Cape Elizabeth. Now I see the streets—Ocean House Road, Two Lights Terrace, and on and on—with their new houses, and I wonder if I could refuse such an address. Isn't that what I want, to be able to live close to my treasure? Isn't that what we all want? Isn't that, I am forced to admit, as I sit on my bench and gaze out over the blue, blue water, the problem?

2001

A History in

Concrete

BLAINE HARDEN

OWN IN THE BOWELS OF GRAND COULEE DAM, YOU can feel the industrial-strength menace of the Columbia. The river, as it pounds through turbines, causes an unnerving trembling at the core of the largest chunk of concrete on the continent. Vibration jolts up from the steel flooring, through shoes and up legs, and lodges at the base of the spine, igniting a hot little flame of panic. The gurgle of water creeping through seams in the dam doesn't help.

Grand Coulee Dam won't hold still. And it does leak. Water sluices noisily through drainage galleries that line the fourteen miles of tunnels and walkways inside the dam. Engineers say all dams leak, they all tremble. It is absolutely harmless, completely normal, nothing to worry about. I don't trust engineers.

This gray monstrosity gives me the creeps. It has ever since I was ten, when my uncle Chester took me on a dam tour, fed me extra-hot horseradish at a scenic restaurant, and laughed until he cried when I spat out my burger. Ever since I learned from my father at the dinner table that this mile-wide monolith was the rock upon which our middle-class prosperity was built. Ever since I worked here in college and got myself fired.

The dam sits out in the middle of nowhere—the tumble-weed coulee country of north-central Washington, a wind-swept landscape of basalt cliffs and grayish soil. Seattle is a 240-mile drive west across the Cascade Mountains, which scrape moisture from the sky and leave the country around the dam in a rain-shadow desert. When construction began, *Collier's* magazine described the dam site as so hell-like that "even snakes and lizards shun it." For as long as I can re-member, I have kept coming back to this unhandsome land to feel the addictive tingle of being near an object that is in-timidating and essential and big beyond imagining.

And it is big. The Bureau of Reclamation, which built Grand Coulee in the 1930s in its crusade to turn every major Western river into a chain of puddles between concrete plugs, loves to talk bigness. The dam is so big, the bureau said, that its concrete could pour a sixteen-foot-wide highway from New York City to Seattle to Los Angeles and back to New York. So big that if it were a cube of concrete standing on a street in Manhattan, it would be two and a half times taller than the Empire State Building. As Franklin D. Roo-sevelt, who ordered the dam built, boasted, "Superlatives do not count for anything because it is so much bigger than any-thing ever tried before."

It was a tonic for the Great Depression and a club to whip Hitler, a fist to smash the private utilities monopolies and a fountainhead for irrigated agriculture. The dam was a glori-ously mixed metaphor validating the notion that God made the West so Americans could conquer it. Grand Coulee's tur-bines came on-line just as the United States entered World War II. It sated an unprecedented national appetite for elec-tricity—to make, for example, aluminum for B-17 Flying Fortress aircraft at Boeing's Seattle plant and plutonium at the top-secret Hanford Atomic Works downriver. Without the dam, said Roosevelt's successor, Harry S. Truman, "it would have been almost impossible to win this war."

My hometown, Moses Lake, about an hour's drive south of the dam, owed its existence to Grand Coulee. Before the dam, the town was notable for its large jackrabbits and frequent sandstorms. It was a hard-luck town, where farmers worked until they wore themselves out, went broke, and moved away without regrets. Even the town fathers had admitted, before the dam, that Moses Lake had a certain pointlessness about it. As one chamber of commerce brochure put it, "Out of the desert a city was built. Some of the earliest homesteaders and settlers would ask, 'Why?' " When I grew up, the answer to that question was obvious. Everyone knew that life itself—at least life as lived in our prosperous farm community, with subsidized irrigation and the nation's cheapest electricity—would be impossible without the dam.

My father, the out-of-work eldest son of a failed Montana dirt farmer, joined four thousand men who were building the dam in early 1936. Arno Harden was a broom-and-bucket man, working in the gut of the construction site. Dams rise from the bedrock of a river in a series of rectangular pours stacked like dominoes, and before each pour, laborers must tidy up, hose down, and sandblast every surface. Otherwise new concrete will not adhere, and cracks and structural weaknesses could cause the dam to fail. For fifty cents an hour, eight hours a day, six days a week, my father scooped up loose rocks and bits of wire and ensured that Grand Coulee would stand for generations.

He hated it, of course, but he did it until he had saved enough money to go to trade school and learn to be a first-class union welder. He then spent most of his working life building dams and welding at other federal projects along the Columbia. Because of the dams, my family was something other than poor, and I grew up in a handsome lakefront house with a bedroom for me and one for each of my three siblings, a new car in the driveway, and money in the bank for a private college.

The dam, though, meant far more than money to my father. It had been the great adventure of his life. He lived at the construction site during six wild years when it was gluey mud in the winter, choking dust in the summer, and live music all night long. He and his brother frequented an unpainted, false-fronted saloon on B Street—a dirt road thick with card-sharps, moonshiners, pool hustlers, pickpockets, piano play-ers, and a few women who, like everybody else, had come to town for money. An ex-con named Whitey Shannon em-ployed fifteen dime-a-dance girls at the Silver Dollar, where the bartender, Big Jack, tossed out men who got too friendly with the ladies. A sweet-voiced crooner named Curly sang like Gene Autry, and between numbers a skinny kid shoveled dirt from the muddy boots off the dance floor. Mary Oaks, the dam's telephone operator, took calls from B Street nearly every night: "The owners would say, 'We got a dead man over here and would you call the police.' If they weren't dead, of course, they would want a doctor."

As my father explained it at the kitchen table, Grand Coulee was an undiluted good. It may have killed more salmon than any dam in history and destroyed the lives of the Colville Indians, who centered their existence around the fish. It may have launched a dam-building craze that turned America's most powerful rivers into adjustable electricity ma-chines. But that was not what I learned at home. I once asked my father if he thought it might have been a mistake to kill all those fish, dispossess all those Indians, and throttle the river. He did not understand the question.

My first real job was at the dam. Grand Coulee was expanding in the early 1970s, and my father used his connections to get me a summer job as a union laborer. It paid the then princely sum of five dollars an hour. My labor crew cleaned up bits of wire, half-eaten pickles, wads of spat-out chewing tobacco, and whatever else might be left behind by craftsmen higher up on the wage scale. This was the same job that my father had hated in the thirties.

I was nineteen, a rising sophomore at Gonzaga University in nearby Spokane, and very impressed with myself. I told my crew how boring our jobs were and how I could not wait to get back to school. Many of the laborers were middle-aged Indians with families. They kept their mouths shut and their eyes averted from me.

Federal inspectors nosed around after our work, spotting un-picked-up wire and other crimes. They complained to a superintendent, who complained to some other boss, who complained to an unhappy man named Tex, our foreman, who then yelled at me, the loudmouthed college boy. Tex wasn't much of a talker. When he did speak, he had an almost incomprehensible west Texas twang. *Wire* came out as *war.*

"Git off yer ass, pick up that war," he would instruct me after complaints about our cleanup job had trickled down the chain of command. We worked swing shift, four to midnight, near the spillway. The river, swollen in the summer of 1971 with heavy snowmelt from the Canadian Rockies, rioted over the dam twenty-four hours a day in a cascade eight times the volume of Niagara Falls and twice as high. The dam's base was a bedlam of whitewater and deep-throated noise, and when Tex shouted *"war"* in my face, I could never hear him. Along with the racket, cold spray geysered up, slathering the construction site in a slippery haze slashed at night by hundreds of spotlights. The entire dam site—wrapped in the spray and yowl of the river—struck me as a death trap. At weekly safety meetings, I filled out lengthy reports on what I considered to be hazardous work practices.

By my fourth week at the dam, Tex had had enough. He told me at the end of the shift not to come back. He mumbled something about *war* and how I spent too much time on my butt when bosses were around. I slunk away from the river, driving home to Moses Lake after midnight. I barely managed not to cry. My father had paid for the Volvo I was driving, paid the eight-hundred-dollar initiation fee that got me into the Laborers' Union, and paid for a big slice of my college education. He had been shrewd enough to work much of his life for men like Tex without getting canned.

When I got home at 2 A.M., I left a note on the kitchen table. My father would be getting up in three hours to drive back up to Grand Coulee, where he was still a welder. The note said I was sorry for letting him down, which was true. What I did not say was that I was relieved to be away from that dam.

Twenty-three years later, I invited my eighty-two-year-old father to ride with me up to Grand Coulee. I would buy him lunch, and he would tell me everything he could remember about the dam. Like most father-son transactions, the deal favored me. But my father welcomed any excuse to look at the dam.

It was an abnormally hot Saturday in May. Snow in the mountains was melting, and water in the reservoir behind the dam was rising faster than the turbines could swallow. The river had to be spilled, a spectacle that only occurs once every few years. We had no idea this was happening until we drove down into the canyon that cradles the dam. Before we could see anything, we heard the dull thunder of falling water and rushed to the railed sidewalk overlooking the dam's spillway.

The river exploded as it fell, and the dam trembled beneath our feet. We had to shout to talk. At the base of the spillway, three hundred feet below us, the Columbia seethed, boiling up a milky spray in the warm wind and turning a marbled green as it scuffled downstream. The din from the falling river and the vibration from the dam made my father smile. For him, it was a song from the thirties, a snatch of dance-hall music from B Street.

Neither of us had ever said a word over the years about that morning when I left him the note on the kitchen table, and it didn't come up that day, either. He had come into my bedroom before leaving for work and woken me up. He had told me it wasn't my fault that I got fired, although he must have known it was. He had said I was a good son.

Instead, as we stood together on that trembling dam, I told my father that the noise, the vibration, and the height scared me. He said it did not scare him, that it had never scared him.

1996

Swearing by the Sandlot

T HE FIELD WAS AN APPROXIMATE RECTANGLE, WIDENING AT
the lower end, where it tilted gently down to the edge of a
yellow marsh. Railroad tracks crossed the marsh on a stone-
and-cinder causeway. Out beyond, a salt pond spread itself in
an embrace of marsh and woods, and beyond that, shimmer-
ing in the far smoke-blue distance, lay Vineyard Sound. This
was the view, looking out from home plate: marsh, causeway, steel-blue pond, silver-blue ocean.

The grandstand on the third-base side was a low wood of
cherry, birch, and bittersweet vines. On the first-base side a
crumbling paved road wandered down toward the marsh,
then crept away into a shaggy field spiked with cedars and
pitch pines. It was quiet here. Private.

Home plate for as long as I can remember was a square
scrap of plywood, splintered along the edges and coated with
milky white paint. The bases varied from year to year, and
often from game to game: scraps of wood or cardboard, a
broken flagstone, a rolled-up jacket. Someone had found an
old wooden storm door in his garage or cellar, and we
propped it against the hedge behind the plywood plate for a
backstop. The bases and pitcher's mound had been sited un-

scientifically, rough guesses that became binding as teardrop-shaped patches of dirt were carved out of the grass, packing down hard and black over the years.

I lived a half-mile up the road from the sandlot, two minutes by bike. Our house—the original rooms, that is—had been built in 1690 by one of the town's founding settlers, Jonathan Hatch, whose mossy headstone is still legible in the Old Town Cemetery. It was a large, plain house with a steep roof, feathered in weather-grayed shingles. On one side huddled a dark little wood of fir trees; on the other, the granite foundation of a long ago barn hid in the weeds and long grass. The railroad tracks ran past our backyard, and beyond them, rising out of a tangle of field and thickets and stands of swamp maple, was a boarded-up yellow mansion. The neighborhood, like the town of Falmouth itself, was still half wild in the 1950s. All of Cape Cod was like that.

I wonder how much baseball would have been played on our sandlot if it hadn't been for me. Surely not as much. Baseball was my guiding passion. It was, I never doubted, my calling. The game, as the big leaguers played it, was heroism; it was the only future worth aspiring to, worth *living* for, and I set my heart on walking one day in the sunlight of the major leagues. Here, on our makeshift diamond above the marsh, was where my journey began.

In early March, when the ground softened and the light began to change, I'd set the journey in motion. You needed at least three on a team—pitcher, first baseman, fielder—and it was difficult on those raw, gray days before the equinox to persuade even the minimum number to come out and play baseball. I could at least count on Buddy Burrough, our next-door neighbor and my best friend. Buddy was two years younger than I, the perfect companion to my earnestness and sense of destiny: sloppy, obliging, with an amiable grin screwed slantwise up his squint-eyed face. I'd line Buddy up, then work my way around the neighborhood by phone, coaxing, flattering, begging till I had two teams. We'd converge on the windswept khaki-green field, drop our bikes by the road, and choose up sides. The new season had begun.

It was cold. We played in winter coats, in hats with earmuffs. A ball smacking in your glove felt as hard as a rock. The cold bat vibrated in your grip like a live wire. With three on a side an inning lasted forever, and it was established early and never forgotten that everyone who showed up was welcome, regardless of ability. There was an unspoken rule: No one gets teased because he has a weak swing or throws like a girl—no one. The skinny bookworm, the clumsy fat boy, the hood with long hair—they all fielded a position, they all took their cuts, they all counted. If you were here, you were a ballplayer.

The weather warmed, the sides grew, the games turned louder and more boisterous. There were no grown-ups present, there were no girls, and we swore whenever the spirit moved us. We swore when we muffed a ground ball or missed clobbering a pitch down the middle. We swore at nothing, loosing the piquant forbidden words on the spring afternoon out of sheer exuberance and love of life.

Toward the end of May, when the days turned soft and drowsy, Mrs. Leland would call Mr. Burrough, Buddy's father, about the swearing. Mrs. Leland lived in the tall shingled house on the other side of the hedge in back of home plate. We were the plague of her springtime. We chased foul balls into her backyard, into her flower gardens. We dug wild throws out of her hedge, prodding and slashing with our bats. She opened her windows to the advancing spring and heard us out there beyond the hedge, cursing and blaspheming like little mule skinners.

Mr. Burrough would arrive in his gray pickup truck with the concrete-block logo on the door. He owned the Falmouth Cement Company, and the Burroughs had one of the nicest houses in the neighborhood, nestling broad and chalk-white in a woodsy hollow steeped in summer shade. Mr. Burrough was a tall, good-looking man with a perfect part in his jet-black hair. He'd get out slowly and slam the door. The game stopped. We drifted over and stood around him in a half-circle. Buddy hung back, chewing a blade of grass and squinting out toward the water. Waiting for this to be over.

"I guess you know why I'm here," Mr. Burrough would say.

We knew. The field belonged to a homeowners' association, of which Mr. Burrough was an elected officer. We understood dimly that he had some authority here.

"Harry Turner," he said. "I could hear you all the way down at my house."

Harry grinned sheepishly and hung his head. Mr. Burrough smiled, too, in spite of himself. We all liked him. We knew he was just doing his job.

"I'm not going to tell you again," he said. "If there are any more complaints, you guys'll have to find someplace else to play. Got that?"

We assured him we had, and for a few days, maybe a week, an unnatural decorousness fell over the ball field. Then Harry Turner would drop a pop fly or hit an easy one back to the pitcher, and suddenly Harry was his old self again, painting the afternoon with his gaudy language. We began to relax. One by one we reverted to our profane ways, until all traces of Mr. Burrough's visit had disappeared. In a month or two, he'd be back again.

I don't think any of us, if we thought about it at all, really believed that any intelligent adult would prevent us from playing baseball. Not *baseball*. It kept us out of trouble. The neighborhood was safer while Johnny Parent, for instance, was occupied on the sandlot. Johnny lived in a narrow white-clapboard box of a house—dusky inside and sparsely fur-nished—by the intersection where our street, Elm Road, left the Woods Hole Road. He was older than the rest of us; tougher, wiser, more self-reliant. He enthralled us with stories of running with his older brother, Billy, and the notorious Johnny Dumont, how they'd let the air out of the tires of po-lice cars, shot out windows, rung doorbells after igniting bags of fish guts on the doorstep, and run a bra up the flagpole on the village green.

Spike Naylor was another whose interest in baseball wasn't likely to be discouraged by grown-ups who knew him. Even his friends' parents regarded Spike with a certain unease and kept an eye on him when he came over to play. At the age of twelve, Spike weighed 205 pounds. It was a solid 205, a po-tent amalgam of brawn and blubber. It was Spike's destiny in those years to shamble through life breaking things, some-times on purpose, sometimes not. Bicycle wheels bent under him, wobbly chairs gave way. He threw stones and broke windows, threw snowballs and shattered windshields. He broke Kenny Morse's leg, proving that nothing was safe from him, even on the sandlot.

Kenny was a summer kid—from New Jersey, I think. He was precocious, and he liked to exercise his advanced vo-cabulary and agile wit at others' expense. Thin-skinned and lumbering, Spike was a natural target. One gray and sultry July morning Kenny was honing his wit on Spike when the big guy decided enough was enough. He put down his glove and waddled swayingly toward Kenny, who was playing first base in a pair of plaid shorts. His legs were pale and bony. He stood his ground, smiling mordantly, and fired off one last witticism at the train bearing down on him. Without a word, Spike wrapped a blimplike arm around his neck and threw him. They went down together, Spike on top, and we all heard the snap, like a stick breaking across your knee.

Kenny began to yell. *"Ahhh,"* he said. *"Ohhh. Ahhh."* Then he started swearing. Spike climbed off him. Kenny lay on his back, eyes closed, teeth bared, and hollered at the low sky.

The ambulance was there in fifteen minutes. It rolled gingerly out onto the field, gleaming in the dullish pearl-gray light. Kenny's mother had been summoned. She'd come in long, rapid strides and stood now over Kenny, her gaze locked on his pale face as if no one else existed. She never looked at Spike or spoke to him. He sat alone by the hedge, morosely slapping a ball into his glove. He looked sorry. Not repentant, perhaps, but sorry.

A few days later, going by Kenny's house on my bike, I found him on a chair on the front lawn, his leg encased in an enormous cast. The sun was shining. Kenny was reading *Mad* magazine and listening to music on a transistor radio. "If you see that big tub-of-lard Naylor," he said, "tell him no hard feelings."

Kenny's broken leg was the only real injury anybody ever received in all our years on the sandlot. There was some roughhousing, some wrestling; not much. Often at the end of an afternoon we'd sprawl in the grass and smoke dead oak leaves wrapped in brown paper. "Ciggy butts," Harry Turner dubbed these large cone-shaped cigars. The smoke was hot against the roof of your mouth and bitter on the tongue. We'd puff away, trying not to choke, and trade dirty jokes and sto-

ries we'd heard of the wild goings-on at the high school, a remote and glamorous world populated by varsity football play-
ers, dangerous hoods, and beautiful girls. At the time, these
lazy sessions in the grass as the sun crept down the sky interested me only marginally. My mind was still on the ball I'd hit
into the marsh that day, or the one-handed catch I'd made in
deep left. Now, forty years later, the talk and the ciggy butts,
the stillness of the hour, the late sunlight on the field and
marsh and steel-blue pond are what I remember most clearly.

Sometimes a train would go by, a square-ended orange-
and-black diesel pulling several boxcars, or the silver Budd-
car commuter, one or two sections long, finishing its
afternoon run from Boston. The freights puttered slowly by,
in no hurry to get where they were going. We waved, and the
engineer answered with a short blast of the horn.

Then it was dinnertime, and we straggled to our bikes and
rode home. Tomorrow we'd be back, and the next day, and the
next, and each day would seem just like yesterday, and each
year like the one before. The years brought their changes
nonetheless. Johnny Parent no longer came to play ball; at
the school bus stop he said hello with a cool nod, as if he
barely knew us. The trains stopped running. Rust grew on the
rails. The ties rotted—Spike could rip them out with his bare
hands—and weeds and baby pitch pines wriggled up
through the stones and cinders. We no longer smoked ciggy
butts. Smoking now meant Lucky Strikes or Chesterfields,
stolen from parents one or two at a time or purchased by
scruple-free older siblings. Cars entered our postgame conversations; V-8s and four on the floor, Buicks and Caddies
and whitewall tires. Someone brought a copy of *Escapade*
and passed it around. Girls were discussed: their figures, their
willingness to bestow a favor. As if we knew all about it.

.   .   .

BY THE TIME I hit high school, I knew I was never going to be a big-league ballplayer. I wasn't half good enough, for one thing. The dream died painlessly, like falling out of love with someone who will always be a good friend. School sports, homework, girls began to claim my time, and I got on the phone less and less often to coax a ball game out of the neighborhood. The storm door backstop disappeared. The hard, deep-worn patches of dirt at the corners of the diamond sprouted grass and thistles and melted finally into the bottle-green carpet of summer. No one played ball here now. Strangely, no younger generation followed us.

In time, the little wood of firs was cut down and a house built next to the one I'd grown up in. The ruined railroad tracks disappeared under a ribbon-smooth bike path. The yellow mansion beyond the tracks was converted to an apartment building, and today its once-wild acres are strewn with Cape-style houses, winding roads, and dead-end circles.

Twenty or maybe thirty years ago, a house was built on our sandlot. It straddles the field at an angle, an ample house of pea-green clapboard with a mansard roof and built-in garage. Its front door opens onto second base, its backyard is deep center field, and its circular driveway tours the infield. The rhododendrons in front have grown tall and sprawling, with thick knotty trunks, but the house itself looks less settled. Maybe it's the angle of its siting or the absence of trees or the slightly irregular shape of the plot. Nobody would be surprised to hear that kids played ball here once.

I don't remember the year, don't remember how old I was when we played that last game. A June afternoon, let's say. School over, summer just beginning. High hard sky, bright as blue fire. The dark grass spattered with dandelions. Spike walloped one into the marsh and so did I, connecting flush on the thick yellow barrel of my Louisville Slugger, a delicious muffled throb in the hands as the ball rocketed toward the horizon. Harry Turner sidearmed a wild throw over Spike's head at first base, swore profusely, then threw back his head and laughed to see Spike's heavy-legged dash for the ball. Buddy Burrough, who would be dead in ten years— killed on an icy road in the Berkshires—tripped over second base and scrambled up grinning.

Afterward, perhaps, we lolled in the cooling grass and told a few jokes, a few stories. The knees of our blue jeans were shiny and stiff with grass stains. The sun dropped; the shadow of Mrs. Leland's hedge crept out. We picked ourselves up, mounted our bikes, and rode away into the golden evening, never doubting we'd be back again.

1997

Metropolitan Hideaways

PHYLLIS ROSE

Some THIRTY YEARS AGO, WHEN I WAS COLLEGE AGE, I
got into the habit of using the Metropolitan Museum of Art as
a time-and-space machine. My doting and protective parents
made me spend summers at home with them in suburban
New York. I countered by studying languages at Columbia
and traveling much in Manhattan.

Pickings were slim then for a stay-at-home runaway like
me. The Temple of Dendur, the Astor Court, the Shoin Room
from Japan, and the *studiolo* from the Palace of Federico da
Montefeltro were not yet on view. I sought out the cool stone
tapestry-hung walls of the medieval gallery. The light was
dim, in one spot filtered through a stained-glass window.
Large polychrome statues of Madonna and child lined the
aisles. In a giant Byzantine fresco above one door, Christ,
bearded and young, had such a sexy mouth that I later found
myself a boyfriend who looked just like him. At the back, a
fifty-by-forty-foot choir screen from a cathedral at Valencia
created another secret space, the space behind it where the
altar would have been. Sacred spaces, statues of mothers and
babies, stained glass, five-times-lifesize frescoes of hippies—
all seemed exotic to me, a secular girl from the suburbs.

Moreover, in the days before the city was uniformly and reliably air-conditioned, I could escape the summer heat within the thick stone walls and darkness of the medieval gallery.

There was another space inside the museum in those days that had an even more elemental appeal: the narrow corridors of the reconstructed Egyptian tombs, the first thing you see even now when you enter the Egyptian wing. I was not far from the age at which we celebrated Thanksgiving by crawling through haystacks in search of pumpkins, and negotiating the labyrinthine tombs had something of the same appeal. Ultimately, perhaps, it was the appeal of returning to the womb, renegotiating the birth canal, and bursting once again into life and light, all possibility ahead—the appeal, they say, of ancient initiation rites.

I DON'T KNOW who got the idea of incorporating within the Metropolitan Museum architectural spaces along with the more usual two- and three-dimensional works of art: painting and sculpture. It's true that many other museums have such spaces. James McNeill Whistler's Peacock Room is reconstructed at the Freer Gallery in Washington, D.C. There's a William Morris Room at the Victoria and Albert in London. The British Museum displays the Parthenon marbles in a separate room, but the friezes are hung along the walls, converting the masterpiece bas-reliefs, designed to face worshippers as they entered the temple into something more like Western easel paintings. The idea of reconstructing the decorated space rather than just peeling off the decorations is as radical as the idea of cultural exchange between distant and different nations compared to the old rapacious mode of art acquisition that landed the Elgin marbles at the British Museum.

The tale of the Temple of Dendur's emigration from Egypt

to the city of New York may be one of the happiest in the an-
nals of progress and preservation. For two thousand years
this modest temple to Isis and the two sons of a local chief-
tain existed in obscurity in lower Nubia, on the banks of the
Nile. It was an early Roman work, in a generic Egyptian temple style that had not changed for three thousand years—not
a masterpiece, but irreplaceable nonetheless. In the early
1950s, when the government of Egypt decided to build the
Aswan High Dam to regulate the flow of the Nile, the plan
meant that the Temple of Dendur, along with the much more
splendid temples at Abu Simbel and a lot else, would be covered forever by water. The United States joined an international campaign to save the great works at Abu Simbel, which
were cut away from the cliffs they were carved into and
hoisted to a safe location above the new Lake Nasser. The
Temple of Dendur became one of several otherwise-doomed
Nubian monuments offered in gratitude by the government
of Egypt to the various foreign governments that had helped
with the rescue.

If you get to the Metropolitan when it's relatively empty,
the Temple of Dendur can claim you, accepting you, allowing you to imagine ancient Egyptians performing rites of Isis
or eighteenth-century European tourists climbing over the
sand to see the half-buried temple and leaving their names
carved, where we can still see them, high up on the stones.
But at times New York claims the temple, using it as the site
of elegant parties. I myself have eaten gravlax on rye in the
temple's courtyard. At such times Dendur seems another cos-
mopolitan immigrant, easy with its own exoticism—akin to
the Egyptian cabdrivers who double-park at lunchtime to run
into the mosque on Ninety-sixth Street to pray—pleased to
have made it to the Big Apple, pleased to be part of the cultural mix that makes the city great.

Let's take another room. Hardly anyone knows about this one. It's in the Islamic section of the museum, which relatively few people visit. I go there to see rugs, glass, and calligraphy, and once, on my way to look at something else, I discovered the Nur al-Din Room, near the entrance to the Islamic galleries. When I saw it, I thought it was Turkish, because of the raised floor, the covered banquettes around the walls suggesting delicious conversation, the dim light coming through the carved wooden grilles on the windows, and the hexagonal marble fountain in the vestibule. In fact, the room is from Damascus, Syria, circa 1707, and reproduces the space in which a wealthy merchant might have received his friends, reclining, eating fruit, soothed by the sound of the water burbling in the fountain.

Many of the special rooms at the Metropolitan were originally made for male relaxation, study, and friendship, so you could say they serve as proof of male privilege throughout world history. You *could* say that, but why be so contentious. Now, at least, they are here for all of us. The Shoin Room, built by Japanese craftsmen in 1985, reproduces a seventeenth-century reception room at Kangaku-in, a guest residence in a Buddhist temple. The *studiolo* from the palace of Federico da Montefeltro at Gubbio is a jewel box of a library, whose exquisite trompe l'oeil inlay work celebrates all the humanist arts of the Renaissance.

Nevertheless, its woman-friendliness is perhaps a reason that one of my favorite rooms at the Metropolitan is the living room from the Francis W. Little House in Wayzata, Minnesota, designed in 1912–14 by Frank Lloyd Wright. The banquettes of the Nur al-Din Room are translated here into American vernacular, comfortably upholstered and joined by upholstered oak furniture, including built-in bookshelves. The room's calming austerity is similar to that of the Shoin Room.

And over it all presides—as Wright often dictated that it
should—a reproduction of the Winged Victory of Samo-
thrace, showing, I think, both how much he appreciated the
female form and how, in his embrace of reproductions, the
low-cost dissemination of art, he was the soul of American
democracy.

Almost every time I go to the Metropolitan I discover something new. In preparing to write this, I decided I should look
at the Wrightsman Galleries, which feature French and continental rooms of the eighteenth century. I have never been
much interested in those styles, and since I've been to Europe
and seen such rooms in reality, they didn't serve for me the
slightly Disneyland-like function that the rest of the museum
does. But as I made my way from the formal French reception rooms, with their astonishing *boiserie,* to some of the
other rooms, with their simpler plaster decorations, I came
across something I'd never seen and that completely charmed
me: an eighteenth-century storefront of carved wood, a sil-
versmith's shop from the quai de Bourbon in Paris. There it
was, reconstructed somewhere I'm not even sure I could find
again, with its teapots and coffee urns on view in the windows, somewhere in the heart of the museum's first floor.

Do you ever have dreams in which you find rooms you
didn't know existed inside your own house? They are dreams
of sufficiency, the opposite of all those dreams in which you
can't get packed in time or you arrive at the exam without
having done the homework. Almost every time I go to the
museum, I live this pleasant dream. I am not always lucky
enough to discover a large permanent installation I've never
seen before—the Assyrian bas-reliefs, the Tiffany portico, the
Petrie Court, which lets you feel as if you're sitting in a garden at Versailles. But there is always *something new:* an in-

stallation of prints and drawings, a photography show, a special exhibit of Tiepolos, Fragonards, Van Eycks, Picassos, tiles from Susa, Art Deco furniture from France. Some people think of museums as repositories of the unchanging, but my museum is always in flux, different every time you look at it, like nature itself.

WHICH BRINGS ME to my last secret space at the Metropolitan. It's only open seasonally, but when it is open—May to November—it's as good a spot to view the seasons as any moon-viewing pavilion in a Ming scholar's courtyard. It's the roof, officially the Iris and B. Gerald Cantor Roof Garden. Access is by elevator, and when you step out and follow the path, you face south and suddenly confront the cliff face of midtown skyscrapers. Between you and the city is Central Park, whose treetops you look down on, bright green in spring, dark green in summer, orange and rust in the fall. People stand on the rooftop pointing out structures—the George Washington Bridge, the Museum of Natural History, the Citicorp building, the Chrysler building, the Dakota, Beresford, and San Remo—and imparting urban lore: how John Lennon died there, *Rosemary's Baby* was filmed there, and the climactic scene in *Ghostbusters* took place there. It is ostensibly a sculpture garden, and sculpture is displayed—often Rodin; recently Ellsworth Kelly—but it calls for a very great sculptor indeed to compete with the views. Several times I've felt the urge to push a particularly large rectangular Kelly out of the way. It was blocking a much greater work of art.

More and more we learn that in previous ages and in other cultures art had a context—icons in a church, totems before a lodge, frivolous murals in the boudoir, erudite carvings in the library—and that the work of art is flat if the context is stripped away. More and more we learn that the arts can be integrated. More and more we come to appreciate how physical spaces extending over acres can be works of art. The greatest such work anywhere must be Central Park, whose artfully created "natural" space of open meadows, trees, rocks, and lakes—the whole empty, teeming rectangle—pulls together, makes sense of, and renders livable that triumph of uncontrolled artifice, New York City.

It's fitting that the Metropolitan Museum should sit inside Central Park, which sits inside the city: a nesting doll of human creativity, like the wooden matryushkas sold by Russian immigrants on the sidewalk in front of the museum. For inside the Metropolitan (inside Central Park, inside New York), there are little nuggets of other cultures, the ultimate treasures of the nesting doll, other enterable spaces—the Temple of Dendur, the *studiolo,* the Astor Court, the Frank Lloyd Wright Room, the Shoin Room, the Nur al-Din Room— places I return to again and again, both to explore time and space and to escape from them.

1999

Sweet Lorain

MICHAEL DIRDA

E VEN NOW, WHEN I HAVEN'T LIVED IN LORAIN, OHIO, FOR
more than thirty years, I still think of it not only as home but
also as a strangely magical place. Isn't there, after all, a kind
of Iron Age romance to deteriorating industrial towns? Eyes
closed, I see the puffing smokestacks of National Tube, the
slag heaps guarding Black River, those ponderous lake
freighters cautiously docking near the jackknife bridge, and
of course, Lake View Park, with its artillery cannon, rose garden, and giant Easter basket, all on the eroding shores of
the blue and polluted Erie. Even now, I can feel the bumpy
B & O Railroad tracks crossing Oberlin Avenue, touch the
soft accumulation of grit on cars parked along Pearl Avenue,
taste the cherry vanilla at the long-gone Home Dairy Ice
Cream Company. So many places there linger in the memory—St. Stanislaus Church, where Polish fishermen attended
5 A.M. mass, the Czech Grill, the Abruzzi Club, the Slovak
Hall, Pulaski Park. Who can doubt that I grew up in what sociologists would quickly label "a classic midwestern Rust Belt
city"?

Sweet Lorain—as poet Bruce Weigl called it in his recent
book of poems. Nobel Prize winner Toni Morrison was born

and educated there, and so was General Johnnie Wilson, the highest-ranking African American in the U.S. military until his retirement. Comedian Don Novello, a.k.a. Father Guido Sarducci, grew up there. My high school was named after favorite son Admiral Ernest J. King, commander of the fleet during World War II. It was rumored that Admiral King High School boasted—*le mot juste*—the highest rate of juvenile delinquency in the state. Might well have been true, since many of my classmates belonged to "clubs" such as Bachelors, Dukes, Barons, Cavaliers, Southerners (denoting South Lorain), Islets, Stylers (for guys with a particular interest in souped-up cars), and Bishops (black kids only). There were girl gangs, too—Emeralds, Rainbows, Debs, Junior Gems. And at least a third of AKHS was African American or Hispanic: Following the Second World War, U.S. Steel had recruited five hundred Puerto Ricans to come work at National Tube. Need I say that we fielded powerhouse football and basketball teams? Go, Admirals!

INDUSTRIAL EMPIRE IN OHIO'S VACATIONLAND—so proclaimed a sign as one entered the Lorain city limits. It's not there anymore. I suppose the local solons realized how ludicrous it must have seemed, after Thew Shovel moved away and American Shipbuilding shut down and Japan's Kobe Steel bought National Tube, reducing a workforce of 13,000 to 2,000, and Lake Erie was declared unsafe for bathing and its perch and white bass too dangerous to eat. But, amazingly, Lorain seems to have survived. As Ohio's "International City," there's still a festival each year, with an international princess and a fair where one can eat kielbasa and piroghi and souvlaki and tacos and cannoli. One year, booths sold T-shirts emblazoned with your choice of ethnic heritage: I'M POLISH AND PROUD; I'M ITALIAN AND PROUD; I'M MEXICAN AND PROUD. Little wonder that I was at least twelve before it dawned on me that not everyone in the world was Catholic.

Almost everybody's father was a laborer, putting in long, sweaty hours on the line at the Ford assembly plant or down at the mill, as National Tube was called. Many men worked turns, seven to three one week, three to eleven the next, eleven to seven following that—and most leaped at the chance to earn time and a half for an extra four or eight hours. During a couple of summers I suffered through a grinding routine like this, one year as a bricklayer's helper re-lining vessels and furnaces, another as a laborer in the rolling mill. Everyone knows that steel mills are volcanically hot and perilous, but you have no idea how deafening they are when behemoth machinery is hammering gigantic ingots into long, round pipes. And the air! Sometimes I could see graphite par-ticles gently floating around me, and would wade through half an inch of fine gray dust on a floor that had been swept clean eight hours before.

At other times, I used to work in tunnels underground, in a crepuscular half-light, shoveling up loose slabs of steel—the outside scale that had fallen from cooling ingots—and then upend my loaded wheelbarrow into buckets the size of con-version vans, which would be hauled away by distant over-head cranes. Laved with sweat trapped inside green asbestos clothing, often wearing a respirator to protect my lungs, I would occasionally stumble across a mentally retarded coworker sitting in the dark behind a mound of slag, talking excitedly to imaginary companions. For one memorable week, in this realm of Moloch, I even debated election and damnation with a young born-again fundamentalist, who had dreams of going to Bible college.

To me, it was all overpowering, awesome, even sublime—

but I knew I wouldn't be spending my life there, as my father had and his father before him. Yet sometimes, at two or three in the morning, I'd find myself high up in "4-Seamless" or one of the other sections of the plant, and I'd look out at the stacks with their flaming gases, smell the rotten-egg odor of the pickling vats, and survey the Piranesi-like ramparts and ladders and rusting buildings. One felt like Satan surveying the immeasurable expanse of hell. What better place, I thought, to argue about free will and the afterlife?

For religion was important in Lorain, which had once been called Ohio's "city of churches." In the summer there were church picnics, with Tilt-A-Whirls, raffles, and seared pigs or sheep slowly roasting on revolving spits. One day a year, the priest would come to bless your house, accept a cup of coffee, and taste your nutroll. Sad-eyed ladies of the Altar Society would clean and decorate for holy days. Serious children, in ill-fitting suits or pretty, ruffled white dresses, would march in processions to receive their first holy communion, or the Knights of Columbus would parade in uniform and salute with uplifted swords. Someone would always faint during midnight mass, finally overcome by the incense. Naturally, there were fish fries on Friday at the K of C hall. On Ash Wednesday half the townspeople sported gray smudges on their foreheads.

At Christmas, families would gather at the union headquarters—the AFL-CIO—and hear rousing speeches, especially if a strike threatened, then sing carols and line up to receive a special gift from Santa. In the evenings one might go shopping downtown, already starting to decay by the mid-1960s, and buy some Faroh's chocolates or stop at the Ohio, Tivoli, or Palace for a movie. Back in the 1920s a tornado had touched down one Saturday afternoon, killing fifteen moviegoers at the State, as the Palace was then called. Those who survived would talk about it all their lives. Out at the first big shopping center, called O'Neill's after its department store, year after year one could chat with a gigantic talking Christmas tree.

Afterward, a father might drive his wife and sleepy children around the town so that they could *ooh* and *aah* at all the lights and decorations. At holidays, mothers would cook all morning and take stuffed cabbage or *lekvar* cookies on afternoon social calls that would sometimes last into the evening. Uncles would drink shots and beers, grow jovial, then start dealing poker around a kitchen table. Little kids would play tag or hide-and-seek, teenagers might flirt, and I, a bookish little boy, would plop down in a corner and read about Tarzan while munching on a ham sandwich with sweet pickles, as happy as I will ever be. Sometimes my uncle Henry would take out his battered concertina, and we would all dance or pretend to dance in his kitchen. At other enchanted times, an older cousin might show off his new bow or .22 rifle, and even allow a four-eyed pipsqueak to sight down its smooth, black barrel.

To wander around Lorain was always an adventure. A kid could climb on his bike and cover the entire town in a single summer afternoon. You might start by pedaling up to the shanty in Central Park, where you could sign out basketballs, checkerboards, and frames for weaving pot holders or lanyards. Then you might race up to Hawthorne Junior High, where I once received not one but two black eyes in a street fight with a kid named Andy. Then over to Broadway, past the Music Center, where we all took accordion lessons, and up toward Rusine's Cigar Store, where you could buy racy paperbacks wrapped in cellophane, and on to Cane's Surplus, where a boy might admire the folding slingshots and stilettos.

By crossing the jackknife bridge to the east side, you could swing by the shipyards and then take the long vertiginous span of the Twenty-first Street bridge and peer down at the inky water of the river or across to the mountains of slag and coke. Afterward, you might turn up Twenty-eighth Street, lined with ethnic bars, tailor and shoe-repair shops, and mom-and-pop eateries. If you went far enough, traveling under the rail overpass, you'd ride into South Lorain, up to the aging YMCA, a monumental redbrick building. From near there you could sometimes glimpse elephantine Euclid trucks lumbering around inside the mill, but before long you'd probably set out for Pearl Avenue to stop at Clarice's Values, the apotheosis of all possible junk shops, from which Clarice herself would sell you, for a mere fifty cents, all the books you could carry away. Then past St. Vitus Church, where we played on the steps before Saturday catechism class, on to dilapidated Oakwood shopping center, and then, probably, a turn down one of the graveled side roads.

On one lived my uncle Steve and aunt Anna; on another, Uncle Henry and Aunt Alice. This latter house gloried in a paradise of rusting steel—old cars, broken engines, metal barrels, bindles of wire—and a chicken shed and a park-size swing set. In the summers I would visit my slightly older cousin Henry, and we would trudge up to the railroad tracks a quarter-mile away and bring back, in wooden wheelbarrows, hunks of coal, scraps of lumber, or even lengths of railroad tie for my uncle's wood-burning furnace. In exchange, he would disburse a nickel pack of BBs for each load—at least until this foolish soul plinked out the streetlight in front of the house. It was a particularly important light, because it

helped illuminate the grassy corner lot where half the neighborhood would assemble for softball games on soft summer
nights.

Does all this sound idyllic? Well, it should. Bliss was it in
Lorain to be alive, but to be young was very heaven. Even
adolescence was intermittently endurable. Playing cards on
Friday evenings in Lethargy Hall, as we called my friend Ray's
basement; cruising up and down Broadway in our friend
Tom's 1964 GTO, L'il Blue Tiger; necking ecstatically in Lake
View Park with a Saturday night date—how could anyone
better spend the confused and angst-ridden years of high
school? All around my friends and me the great world
hummed, but Lorain remained its own place, homey and
human-scale, living for football games at George Daniel Field
and carnivals at shopping centers and parades on the Fourth
of July and long, slow beers sipped by tired steelworkers
slouching in Adirondack chairs in oak tree–shaded back-
yards.

Certainly, I mythologize. Perhaps more than a bit. Childhood can be a golden age no matter where it is spent. And
yet. Toni Morrison regularly goes back to Lorain and in interviews expresses a similar affection for the place. Fifteen or
more years ago, Gloria Emerson contributed an article about
the city to *Vanity Fair* and later told me how much she envied anyone who could grow up in such a sturdy, honest
world. And, of course, I return there still, to see my widowed
mother and my sisters. My own children spend part of their
summers in Lorain with their cousins, wonderful days of
baseball and hide-and-seek and swimming, and at the end of
every visit they always say to me, "Dad, why can't we live in
Lorain? Why do we have to go back to stupid, dull Washington?" I never quite know what to tell them. Doubtless their

parents would go crazy after a couple of weeks, and obviously I have a job and their mother has a job and clearly there are a dozen really good reasons not to be in Lorain. But even now I sometimes wonder: Could I go back home, back to this ardently beloved, industrial Eden? Probably not. But like other exiles from paradise, I can still quietly murmur that, at least once, "I too lived in Arcadia."

2000

ROBERT WILSON has been the editor of *Preservation,* the magazine of the National Trust for Historic Preservation, since 1996. In 1998 *Preservation* won the National Magazine Award for general excellence. Wilson is the former literary editor of *Civilization* magazine and book-review editor for *USA Today.*

ABOUT THE CONTRIBUTORS

STANLEY ABERCROMBIE, a contributing editor of *Preservation,* is a retired architect and former editor in chief of three design magazines. His most recent book is *Interior Design and Decoration.*

ANN BEATTIE is the author of fourteen books, most recently *The Doctor's House.* She is a contributing editor of *Preservation.*

MADISON SMARTT BELL's most recent novel is *Anything Goes.* He is the author of ten other novels, including a 1995 National Book Award finalist, *All Souls' Rising,* and two story collections.

SUDIP BOSE is associate editor of *Preservation.*

FREDERICK BUSCH's twenty-fifth book, the novel *A Memory of War,* will be published in February 2003. His latest novel is *The Night Inspector;* his latest story collection is *Don't Tell Anyone.*

JAMES CONAWAY is a contributing editor of *Preservation* and the author of many books, most recently *The Far Side of Eden.*

WAYNE CURTIS is a freelance journalist and contributing editor of *Preservation.* He's the author of several travel guides, and his stories have appeared in *The New York Times, Atlantic Monthly, House Beautiful,* and *Yankee.*

ANITA DESAI is the John E. Burchard Professor of Writing at MIT and the author of *In Custody, Baumgartner's Bombay,* and *Fasting, Feasting,* among other books.

MICHAEL DIRDA, a writer and senior editor of *The Washington Post Book World,* received the 1993 Pulitzer Prize for criticism. The author of *Readings: Essays and Literary Entertainments,* he is finishing a book about growing up in Lorain, Ohio.

BRIAN DOYLE is the editor of *Portland Magazine* at the University of Portland, in Oregon. He is the author of the essay collections *Credo* and *Saints Passionate and Peculiar.* His essays have appeared in *American Scholar, Atlantic Monthly, Commonweal, The Georgia Review, Harper's,* and *Orion.*

SUZANNE FREEMAN, a contributing editor of *Preservation,* is the author of a novel, *The Cuckoo's Child.*

STEPHEN GOODWIN is the author of the novels *Kin, The Blood of Paradise,* and the forthcoming *Love Comes Over You.*

MORRIS HALLE retired from teaching in the MIT Department of Linguistics and Philosophy in 1996. He continues to do research in his specialty, the sounds of language.

BLAINE HARDEN is a national reporter for *The New York Times.* He lives in New York.

EDWARD HOAGLAND's most recent book is a memoir, *Compass Points.* Among his many other books are the essay collections *Walking the Dead Diamond River* and *The Tugman's Passage,* the travel book *African Calliope,* and the novel *Seven Rivers West.*

ROY HOFFMAN is the author of the novels *Chicken Dreaming Corn,* which has just been published, and *Almost Family.* A collection of his nonfiction, *Back Home: Journeys Through Mobile,* was published in 2001.

JOHN HOUGH, JR., grew up on Cape Cod and now lives in the town of West Tisbury on Martha's Vineyard. His most recent novel is *The Last Summer.*

DAVID HUDDLE is the author of *The Story of a Million Years* and *La Tour Dreams of the Wolf Girl.* He teaches at the University of Vermont and the Bread Loaf School of English.

MAURICE ISSERMAN is the William R. Kenan Professor of History at Hamilton College. His books include a number of studies of American politics, reform, and radicalism, including most recently *The Other American: The Life of Michael Harrington.* He is writing a history of mountaineering.

MALCOLM JONES is a senior writer at *Newsweek* and a frequent contributor to *Preservation.*

KATE LEHRER's most recent novel, *Out of Eden,* won the Western Heritage Award. Her fourth novel will be published in 2003. She grew up in Texas and now lives in Washington, D.C.

REEVE LINDBERGH is the author of *Under a Wing: A Memoir; No More Words: A Journal of My Mother, Anne Morrow Lindbergh;* and *In Every Tiny Grain of Sand: A Child's Book of Prayers and Praise.*

THOMAS MALLON is a novelist and critic. His books include *Henry and Clara, Two Moons,* and *In Fact: Essays on Writers and Writing.*

PAUL MARIANI is a poet, critic, biographer, and teacher. His most recent books are *Thirty Days: On Retreat with the Exercises of St. Ignatius* and *God and the Imagination: On Poets, Poetry, and the Ineffable.*

JAN MORRIS has written some forty books and says she will write no more. They include a major work of British imperial history, the Pax Britannica trilogy, studies of Wales, Spain, Venice, Oxford, Manhattan, Sydney, and Trieste, two autobiographical works, two capricious biographies, five volumes of collected travel essays, a novel, and a short book about her own house in Wales.

JAY PARINI is a poet and novelist who teaches at Middlebury College. His most recent novel is *The Apprentice Lover,* and he is currently editing *The Oxford Encyclopedia of American Literature.*

EDITH PEARLMAN is the author of two collections of short stories, *Vaquita* and the forthcoming *Love Among the Greats.* Her nonfiction has appeared in *The New York Times, Atlantic Monthly, Smithsonian,* and *Preservation.*

NOEL PERRIN is an adjunct professor of environmental studies at Dartmouth College. He has been building and rebuilding stone walls for the last thirty years.

PHYLLIS ROSE is an essayist and a literary critic who has taught for many years at Wesleyan University.

SCOTT RUSSELL SANDERS, a writer of essays, novels, and children's stories, is Distinguished Professor of English at Indiana University. His most recent books are *Hunting for Hope, The Country of Language,* and *The Force of Spirit.*

ANTHONY WALTON is the author of *Mississippi: An American Journey* and coeditor of *The Vintage Book of African American Poetry: 200 Years of Vision, Struggle, Power, Beauty, and Triumph from 50 Outstanding Poets.* A recipient of a 1998 Whiting Writer's Award, he teaches at Bowdoin College.

This book was set in Garamond, a typeface originally designed by the Parisian typecutter Claude Garamond (1480–1561). This version of Garamond was modeled on a 1592 specimen sheet from the Egenolff-Berner foundry, which was produced from types assumed to have been brought to Frankfurt by the punch-cutter Jacques Sabon.

Claude Garamond's distinguished romans and italics first appeared in *Opera Ciceronis* in 1543–44. The Garamond types are clear, open, and elegant.